REDEMPTION MOTIFS IN FAIRYTALES

Marie-Louise von Franz, Honorary Patron

**Studies in Jungian Psychology
by Jungian Analysts**

Daryl Sharp, General Editor

MARIE-LOUISE VON FRANZ

The Psychological Meaning of
REDEMPTION MOTIFS
IN FAIRYTALES

Canadian Cataloguing in Publication Data

Franz, Marie-Louise von, 1915-
    The psychological meaning of redemption motifs
in fairytales

(Studies in Jungian psychology)
Based on a series of lectures given in 1956 at the C.G. Jung
Institute in Zurich, Switzerland.
Includes index.

ISBN 0-919123-01-5

1. Fairy tales — History and criticism.
2. Redemption in literature.   3. Psychoanalysis
and literature.   4. Jung, Carl Gustav, 1875-1961.
I. Title.   II. Series.

GR550.F72   398'.042   C80-094434-8

INNER CITY BOOKS
Box 1271, Station Q, Toronto, Canada M4T 2P4

Honorary Patron: Marie-Louise von Franz.
Publisher and General Editor: Daryl Sharp.
Editorial Board: Fraser Boa, Daryl Sharp, Marion Woodman.

INNER CITY BOOKS was founded in 1980 to promote the understanding
and practical application of the work of C.G. Jung.

Cover: Woodcut from the alchemical text, *Rosarium Philo-
sophorum*, 1550, illustrating the motif of immersion in the
bath.

Set in Baskerville by Blain Berdan, Toronto
Printed and bound in Canada

CONTENTS

Please see final pages for *Catalogue and Order Form*

This book is based on the transcription by Miss Una Thomas of the lecture series presented by Dr. von Franz at the C.G. Jung Institute, Zürich, in the fall of 1956. The author and publisher are grateful to Miss Thomas for her faithful preparation of the original version. The text in its present form was edited for publication by Daryl Sharp and Marion Woodman. The index was compiled by Daryl Sharp.

Lecture 1

The word redemption should not be associated with the Christian dogma and theology, where it is a concept with so many connotations. In fairytales, redemption refers specifically to a condition where someone has been cursed or bewitched and through certain happenings or events in the story is redeemed. This is a very different condition from that in the Christian idea.

The type of curse can vary. A being in a myth or fairytale is generally condemned to assume an animal form or to be an ugly old woman or man who, through the process of redemption, turns into a prince or princess again. There are certain types of cold and warm-blooded animals, frequently the bear, the wolf or lion, or birds—the duck, the raven, dove or swan, or owl—or it may be a snake. In other cases someone is cursed and thereby forced to do evil and be destructive, without desiring to act in this manner. For instance, a princess has to kill all her lovers, but in the end, when redeemed, she will say that the curse forced her into such behaviour, but that is now over. These are the main types of evil fate which befall a person in a fairytale and from which he or she is redeemed.

I have chosen not to lecture on a particular fairytale, but to discuss motifs from various tales showing the different types of curses, because I think they have an important psychological meaning, as well as often being the main theme. A human being in a neurotic state might very well be compared to a bewitched person, for people caught in a neurosis are apt to behave in a manner uncongenial and destructive towards themselves as well as others. They are forced onto too low a level

7

of behaviour and act in an unconscious, driven way. Fairytales which describe such beings do not dwell much on the problem of the curse, but on the method of redemption, and here there is much to learn that is relevant to therapeutic procedures and the healing process.

To give a general example, there are bewitched beings who have to be bathed in water or milk and sometimes beaten at the same time. Others ask to be beheaded, as when the head of the fox or lion is cut off; others have to be loved or kissed, or have to eat flowers, and so on. Or a certain kind of skin has to be thrown over the person, or the animal skin has to be put on, or questions have to be asked, or not asked. These are the types of motifs that we must consider.

It frequently occurs in therapy that doctors hope to find recipes and formulas, but, in contrast to other schools of psychology, Jungians always say they are sorry but there is no recipe for types of illnesses. Each case is a unique process surrounding a unique individual, and the individual way is always different. Under such conditions we can say that we have no therapeutic recipe. Therefore we cannot discuss it in general in a lecture, we can only advise people who have control cases how they should behave with the unique patient. In this very difficult situation, in which the doctor or analyst has no guiding rules for the cure of his patient, we have dream interpretation, and we believe that if we interpret the dreams of the patients carefully and objectively, without putting in our own theories, we can get a hint as to how to proceed.

Thus the only theoretical help or guidance we have is the capacity to objectively and accurately interpret the dream motifs so that we can see how the unconscious proposes to effect a cure. Here we enter a field which is not only individual, for though the healing process is always unique, fairytales and myths give representations of instinctive processes in the psyche which have a general validity. Just as, in spite of differences, human beings all walk on two legs, have only one mouth and two eyes, so the human psyche, in spite of differences, has certain basic structural characteristics which can be found everywhere. On that level of the collective unconscious, you find representations of typical processes of cure for typical diseases. If you know in general what a bath for a bewitched person means and the patient dreams that the analysis is compared to a bath then you have an intuitive idea of the type of cure that is proposed. On the other hand, if there is a dream motif of having to cut a being apart, you again have an intuitive view as to the direction of the healing processes and you have some knowledge of how to proceed with the individual case. Naturally, there is always the question as to who is to be bathed, and who is to be beheaded, but such information is usually given in the dream material.

We must therefore look closely at our material and comment on the general problem which makes the understanding of mythological material, especially fairytales, difficult. When you read such a tale naively and with feeling, you will always start with the idea that the person in the centre of the story—the princess, prince, the boy or the girl—is a human being and will identify with it (usually females with females and males with males) and participate in all the suffering. If you read a myth, for instance *The Odyssey* or *The Gilgamesh Epic,* identification is helped by the fact that the hero behaves like a human being: he is afraid, is sad, is happy, and so on. He says: "What shall I do?" etc., and he thus approaches the human realm and one can identify with him. Heroes in myths are more nation-bound than those in fairytales.

It has been pointed out by scientists, and their reasons are convincing, that the hero or heroine is very different in fairytales than in myths. In fairytales they are much less human, that is, they have no inner human life of the psyche. They do not talk to themselves, they have no doubts, do not get uncertain, or have human reactions. There the hero is courageous and never loses courage but keeps on fighting till he overcomes

9

the enemy. The heroine will go on being tortured; she suffers her way through until she reaches her goal. We are never told about any human reactions they may have. Therefore, one of the scientists, Dr. Max Lüthi, goes as far as to say that the heroes in folklore are black and white shapes, they are like clichés, with a very characteristic trend such as cleverness, capacity for suffering, loyalty, etc., and the figures stay so to the end of the story. You will never find anything like a psychological conversion in a fairytale hero, while a change of attitude is often found in a myth. In spite of having very human characteristics, then, these fairytale heroes are not quite human. That is because they are not only types of human beings but archetypes, and therefore cannot be compared directly with the human ego. You cannot take the hero as one man, or the heroine as one woman.

When people have sniffed a little whiff of Jungian psychology, they may be worse than if they knew nothing, for they take a fairytale and a few of the Jungian concepts and pin these on to the figures, e.g., the ego, the anima, the Self. This is worse than no interpretation for it is unscientific, not objective, infantile, and even dishonest, because in order to be able to pin Jungian concepts onto such a being, you are obliged to twist the story. For instance, supposing one is naively caught in an error and pins the quality of the shadow onto one of the fairytale figures, and then finds that it does not work all the way through. Such people will say that then they must have been wrong in the beginning, or that they did not understand quite well themselves, or that there was a mistake in the whole fairytale! Or else they will skip the awkward part with a general statement and skate around it with various ideas to make their concepts fit. If you are careful, you will see that these concepts of Jungian psychology cannot without restriction be used for the interpretation of fairytales. When I discovered this myself I suddenly realized that it must be so because a fairytale is not produced by the psyche of the

10

individual and is not individual material.

Dr. Jung built up his concepts partly through the observation of his own psychic processes, and partly by observing those of others. When we speak of the anima, we think of man as an individual, of the anima of a certain being, or the ego is the ego of a human person, and the shadow means the person's inferior side. But such terms must not be swindled into a tale where they do not belong, and if they have been conceived in the course of the observation of many individuals it is quite questionable whether the concepts can be applied to material like fairytales—material which probably has been produced by many persons, or a group. Therefore we must go back to the basic problem of fairytales. Their origin has not been generally accepted and we may venture one more hypothesis, namely one from the psychological point of view.

Among simple people, for instance peasants and wood cutters, the circle in which nowadays fairytales are mostly set, there are two particular types: the local saga and the real fairytale. The former is very often not very different from the fairytale, but it is generally concerned with a fantastic story which happened at a certain place, or a certain castle. It is said that the people in the village witnessed some particular event there, and so on. The story gets pruned down and pinned on to a certain place, the hero becomes a definite human being, and the tale is spoken of as if it were a definite event which really took place, though it has all the characteristics of a fairytale. In fairytales you often come across parapsychological phenomena while spook elements are more frequent in local sagas. Legends usually have an historical, or partly historical, foundation. Saints or historical personages may figure in them.

In Switzerland, we have the story of William Tell and historians squabble as to whether it is a true story, a fairytale, or saga motif, for such a figure also occurs in Nordic tales, but it still has the pretension of being historical and the events are said to have happened at a certain place and time. From the

11

psychological angle this can be commented upon. It does sometimes happen that in an ordinary human life such fantastic events occur that if you could not check up on them you could think you were being told a fairytale. I have often experienced this, and here we enter on the problem of synchronicity. It is amazing to see how often events like those in a fairytale actually come to pass, if an archetypal situation is constellated. If such a mythological motif occurs it is quite possible that it may be spun out and things added which did not actually occur. Some little thing may be added which makes it much more interesting and one has to realize that this occurs frequently, and a whole mythological event thus becomes crystallized.

I would therefore say that the local saga and the historical legend are both based on actual events that have been experienced and then spun out and extended into a story and thus come to be retold over a long period of time. I have found actual evidence for this theory. In a certain village in the Swiss mountains near Chur, there once lived the family of a miller who owned a book in which family events were narrated. Some descendants of the family now live in Chur and have the old family book in which events which happened to their ancestors 150 years ago are written down. One story is about a miller who meets a spook fox who talks, shortly after which the miller dies. Now this is a widespread motif all through the world: if you meet your bush soul, an animal which can speak, that is an announcement of your fate.

In 1937, a student of folklore asked the old people of the village about the mill, and was told that there was a spook there and given the same story, but partly impoverished and partly enriched, saying how the fox went through the miller's legs causing his death. In that whole region it is believed that a fox represents a witch soul and can produce inflammation of the skin (red fox = red skin), so you see that a generally widespread folklore belief has been added to the original chronicle.

It is also said that the fox was the soul of an aunt of the miller, and that the miller's death was brought about by the witch soul of the aunt. Life in a village is apt to be boring so exciting stories have to be made up.

In such cases you can see how from an individual invasion of consciousness an archetypal image, a local saga, has grown. Further, if such a local saga has a very general character, then it wanders from its original home to neighbouring villages and in migrating loses its local interest. For instance, the original miller had a certain name and lived in a certain place, but with these changed the migrating saga loses the local characteristics which pin it down to a certain time and place and it becomes more general, thereby losing local interest but gaining wider acceptance.

Therefore when we study a fairytale motif we do something like making a comparative anatomy of the human psyche: everything which is individual or local is washed away to a great extent because it is of no interest. In spite of this fact, I shall have to go back on this theory and modify it later, for fairytales are not quite purified of specific factors. If you compare tales, you will see that though there are certain similarities—witches, helpful animals, etc.—the setup of the story is quite different in the fairytale of a North American Indian and that of a European, even though names and places are cut out. To study a myth is like studying the whole body of a nation. If you study a fairytale, it is like studying a skeleton, but I think it shows more basic features in a purer form, and if you want to study the basic structures of the human psyche it is better to study the fairytale than the myth. If we apply this hypothesis, we come back to what I said before, namely that the hero and heroine are not human individuals, but archetypal figures.

When I first tried to push this theory further and tried to teach other people to accept it, I met with great feeling difficulties, and I had to realize that I myself did not like the

13

theory. I had once more to say that I was sure the character in the fairytale was not a human subject, but you cannot get away from the suggestive idea of treating it as a human being. This was the real difficulty for a long time till I came to the conclusion that there must be a general instinctive basis to the ego and that we must assume that there is an inborn tendency of the human psyche which we would call the ego building factor, and which seems to be one of the typical features of the human being.

Now if you study the psychology of children, and I would like to refer you to the papers of Michael Fordham, you will see that the ego can appear projected as though it were "not my ego." Many children talk about themselves objectively by name, and do not say "I," for their "I" is projected into the name. To name the right name is sometimes an important thing: "Johnny has spilt the milk." The feeling experience of identity with the ego is lacking. If you watch you will often find that the next stage of the ego personality is projected into *one* being who is tremendously admired. It may be a school friend whom the child imitates like a slave. You could say that the future form of the ego is projected onto that friend. In such a case it may be said that qualities which later belong to the ego of such a boy are not yet identified, but projected into another being.

Here you see the ego-building factor at work through a fascination which induces imitation. If, on the other hand, you study primitive societies you have the same phenomenon in another form for in these only the king or chief, or the medicine man, has the quality of being individual. In a primitive tribe, if a crime has been committed, a certain man may be proved guilty, yet the blame may be attributed to another who will accept the punishment. This, of course, upsets the missionaries! The psychological explanation is that a crime committed in a tribe has to be punished, but anyone chosen, not necessarily the guilty party, may take the punishment and this is quite in order. Again, should a white man hurt the feelings of one of his black servants, the latter is capable of hanging himself with the idea that this will give his master a shock! That the man dies in giving the shock does not matter, the main thing is the shock given to the other. The ego is so weak that the individual is not important; the main thing is the vengeance. One could say that a patient with a weak ego is in the same position.

If we begin to think about the ego complex, we find it to be a very complicated phenomenon, and have to realize that we know very little about it, though it seems to have certain widespread characteristics. You could make the working hypothesis that the hero in fairytales has a psychological image which demonstrates this ego-building tendency and serves as a model for it. The word "hero" suggests this, for he is a model person. The reaction of wanting to imitate the figure is spontaneous. I will go into this later in more detail.

Study of mythological material by a comparison of heroes and heroines shows that they have very much the same typical characteristics which identify the image, to a great extent, with what Jung calls the archetype of the Self and which he speaks of as being very different from the ego. In the human personality as a whole, the ego is only one part. A large part of the psyche is not identical with the person. Jung defines the self-regulating activity of the whole as the archetypal Self. Identification with the Self, Jung says, is catastrophic, and it is very important to keep the concepts of the Self and the ego apart.

In *Mysterium Conjunctionis,* Jung points out that the unknown factor which builds up the ego complex and keeps it going is really the archetype of the Self. The ego complex has a great continuity. For instance, if I run into something, I remember it the next day. If I have the will power I can keep memories, or an attitude, with complete continuity, and this is one way of measuring the strength of the ego complex. Continuity of thought is typical for a well-developed ego complex

15

and this can be practised. Ego continuity is psychologically a very mysterious thing. One could say that this strong quality of continuity, which the ego complex of a human being seems to develop, is supported by the archetype of the Self.

Thus when we interpret fairy stories there is the constant difficulty of how to explain the main figures in the story. If the figure behaves like the ego, or the Self, you can get off the track. Therefore I call it *that part of the archetype of the Self which is the model of the ego complex and its general structure.* One of the main functions of the archetypal Self is to support ego consciousness and this right kind of continuity. If you take the human personality as a sphere, with the Self embracing the whole sphere and also being the self-regulating factor in the centre, any deviation will have compensations. We notice such manifestations in dreams. If you have a destructive affect against another person, you may dream of throwing something at that person and you take this warning, for dreams comment on what you do. You may have long periods without any dreams, but if you are in danger of deviating from your own totality you will get them. The health of the individual is best when the ego complex functions in tune with the Self, for then there is a relative minimum of neurotic disturbances.

In fairytales either the hero or the heroine is cursed, so that the person has to behave in a destructive, negative way and it is the task of the hero to redeem the bewitched person. We can say that any archetypal complex, any structural unity of the collective unconscious psyche, can be cursed or bewitched; it need not be the hero and could therefore be any other complex. We must always look carefully to see which factor has been bewitched or cursed. In general we can say that this can be compared with a neurotic state. According to the tales a curse is often inflicted without cause. It is a state into which one gets involuntarily, generally innocently, or where there is

16

guilt it is of a minor nature like the story of the apple in the Garden of Eden.

Where there is guilt in a fairytale it is of a seemingly minor kind due to which the curse falls on the figure. There is, for instance, the Grimm fairytale "The Seven Ravens." In this story the father sends his sons for water to baptise their sister and they break the vessel in which they were to bring the water. In his vexation, the father says that he wishes the boys were all ravens, and the boys turn into ravens and their sister has to redeem them. Guilt of this kind is sometimes mentioned, but generally there is no explanation of the curse. The tale usually begins with the statement that there is a bewitched princess, without any explanation or reason being given for the curse. Another theme is that of an ugly witch who makes love to a beautiful prince who refuses her, and one of the two curses the other who may be turned into an animal.

Primitive societies live in constant fear of bewitchment. It is something which may happen to anyone at any time, without the person being at fault. Cows, for instance, may have no milk, which may happen to anybody's cows. If you put that into psychological language, one might say that an impulse forces us into a wrong attitude so that we become alienated from our instincts and lose our inner balance. Through inherited character one can be pushed into such situations. You may love adventure, but you cannot live an adventurous life if you are over-sensitive. Thus the human being is born with contradictory impulses.

In psychological terms one could compare a person in a fairytale who is bewitched to someone in whom one structural entity of the human psyche has been damaged in its functioning and is unable to function normally. The complexes all influence each other. If a man's anima is neurotic, though the man himself is not, he will feel himself to be partly bewitched. In dream life you can see this. I woke up one morn-

17

ing and said "Goodbye" to the world, for I thought I was going to die. I was not unhappy. The strange mood lasted the whole day. I looked at flowers sentimentally, I was kind to everybody, it was all more romantic than anything else. The next night I dreamt that a very romantic boy actually did die. Therefore what died was a kind of infantile animus, and it was quite time that he went, but his dying "Goodbye" mood affected my whole psyche. That is typical.

You may say of people that they are not wholly neurotic but one complex is ill, and therefore to a certain extent the whole person is ill. There is sometimes a neurotic complex within a normal person. One complex is affected and has a neurotic effect on the rest of the person and that accounts for the different degrees of neuroses. On the other hand, where certain complexes are affected, an otherwise normal person may be completely mad. In general, to be bewitched means that one particular structure of the psyche is crippled or damaged in its functioning and the whole is affected, for all complexes live, so to speak, within a social order given by the totality of the psyche and this is why we are interested in the motif of bewitchment and its cure.

Lecture 2

Last time we discussed which character filled the role of the hero in a fairytale, and we came to the conclusion that it is impossible to make a comparison of the hero with the ego of the human being. The hero in the fairytale rather represents that aspect of the Self which is concerned with the building up of the ego, with keeping it going and enlarging it. He is also an archetypal model and pattern for the right kind of behaviour.

However, comparison of one tale with another shows a great variety in this respect. Some heroes may just sit over the stove and yawn and apparently achieve nothing, but they end in marrying the princess, while others may have to overcome brigands and witches, etc. Nevertheless, when you read a fairytale you have the feeling that this is the right way, that only through this particular kind of behaviour could the hero reach his goal while everybody else missed it. Thus, in some cases it is right to be stupid, while in others the hero has to be very clever or heroic. Sometimes magic is required, or the helpful animal, while another time the hero does the task alone. There always seems to be a typically right behaviour. If you participate with your feeling, you have the idea that this is the right way to do it and through this identification you feel that this is the secret way in which to meet life. One can therefore say that the behaviour of the hero can only be understood within the whole setup of the story, and that he represents the person whose instinctive action is right in this specific situation.

But what *is* the "right" kind of behaviour? This is one of the difficulties in fairytales, for they are so naively convincing that one does not question them. Obviously the hero's behaviour does not conform to the ordinary civilian's standards; he can be stupid, naive, or cruel and use all kinds of tricks which we would condemn, yet however he behaves, you still have the feeling that he is right. Therefore this "rightness" could perhaps be better defined as being in complete accordance with the wholeness of the situation. You can never say, "All right, brigands have to be slain and witches always have to be outwitted," for you can always find other stories where this is not so. Thus no recipe is possible. You can only say that in *this* story it is obvious from the outcome that the hero did the right thing, though no one could have guessed what he had to do next, for what the hero does is always a surprise. Therefore this kind of getting at the right possibility is something much more primitive than an intellectually right attitude; it comes from the depths of the personality and is in accordance with the Self. In this way it illustrates a fact which we can also observe in psychologically difficult individual situations, namely that there is no conventional answer to an individual complex.

Usually an analysand who comes into analysis has tried out what could be done in general in the conscious situation, and you are therefore confronted with the ticklish question left us by society of finding out what the person in his particular conditions ought to do, and here we can say that the "right" behaviour can be described as that which is in accordance with the totality of the psychological personality. The situation in fairytales is similar, for hero and heroine may be said to represent models for a functioning of the ego in harmony with the totality of the psyche. They are models for the healthy ego, an ego complex which does not disturb the total setup of the personality, but which normally functions as its organ of expression.

Compared with other warm-blooded animals, the human being is unique in that it has developed a specific focussed form of consciousness not to be found in other beings, at least not on this planet. Animals seem to be bound to their patterns of

20

behaviour to a much greater extent, often even to the point of destruction. For instance, lemmings (small arctic rodents, something like field mice and also akin to squirrels), like many other animals, tend to form into groups from time to time and migrate. Obviously, nature endowed animals with this instinctive urge so as to compel them to change their feeding places and not eat up everything in one place. This instinct of migration is so strong that they move straight ahead, even into a stream where they are drowned. They are incapable of stopping and going another way. Thus animals cannot detach from their pattern of behaviour even though it may destroy them.

The human being, however, has a much greater capacity for adaptability and can live in all climes all over the world and in conditions to which he was not born. But for this he has paid a great price, for through this much greater adaptability and the capacity for going against his own animal instincts, he is able to repress these instincts to such an extent that he becomes neurotic, and the whole of the personality cannot function any longer. This is the heavy price man pays for his greater freedom. Therefore the human ego is also confronted with the temptation to deviate from the instincts to such an extent that difficulties may arise. It is therefore tremendously important for human consciousness to have a model in mind, a pattern as to how the ego can function in accordance with the rest of the instinctual conditions. The hero in myths and fairytales has this function of reminding one of the right way of behaving in accordance with the totality of the human being. That there are many possibilities only shows the difficulty of the task.

The first motif of redemption which I want to discuss is that of the bath. This is a very widespread technique of redemption. In many fairytales there is the motif of the cursed or bewitched being, either male or female, who is condemned to evil doing and who can be redeemed by taking some kind of bath. It may be just a bowl of water into which the hero may have to push his partner three times, thus affecting redemption, or the liquid may be the milk of a cow or the urine of a horse. The temperature of the bath may not be mentioned, or it may be a kind of sweat bath of very high temperature, or perhaps the being who is under a curse may have to be cooked in the water. Sometimes there is the motif of the stove instead of the bath, but that we will take separately.

An example of the bath procedure is contained in a Norwegian fairytale called "The Comrade" in which the princess is in the clutches of a mountain demon, a very old man with a white beard. He is the secret lover of the princess and together they hatch the idea that the princess shall lure men into her net and set them riddles. If the solution to the riddle is not found, the man is beheaded, with the result that the princess kills all her suitors, whether she enjoys doing so or not. In another variation she has a trollskin. (According to the Oxford dictionary, a troll is a "supernatural being, giant or (later) friendly but mischievous dwarf, in Scandinavian mythology.") In both cases, a hero appears who has a ghostly helper to tell him how to behave. This being has wings and can fly to the place where the plots are hatched and can listen while the old devil and the princess decide upon the riddles, so that he is able to give the answer to the questions. Through this he depotentiates the evil in the princess and she agrees to sleep with him and accepts him as her husband, but then the ghostly person says that the battle has not been won and that the princess will destroy the hero on their wedding night unless he prepares a bowl of water and dips her in it three times.

In the Germanic version the dipping is described as the placing of a bowl of water near the bed so that when the princess jumps up in the night with the intention of running away, she falls into the water. The princess has then to be caught and a raven flies out and tries to escape, and then a dove, which has

22

also to be pushed into the water, after which the princess appears in her true form and can safely be married. In the Nordic version the danger is terrible. The hero goes to bed and pretends to be asleep. The princess tried to find out whether he is really asleep and takes a knife to kill him, but he catches hold of her and whips her with hazel rods until they break. Then he washes her first in sour and then in sweet milk, after which her trollskin falls off, together with her evil intentions. In this variation, she would not only have run away but would have killed the man on her wedding night. There is the same motif in the apocryphal Book of Tobit.

Another variation of the same story says that the princess has knives in her body and that through sleeping with her the husband will be killed. The motif of secret weapons in the body of the bride is also found in alchemical texts when exorcism by bath is necessary.

In considering the symbolism of the bath, comparison can be made with all the different baptismal rites which we have in our own religion and in pre-Christian rituals. For instance, in the Eleusynian mysteries the participants went first to the sea to take a ritual bath. Such cleansing baths taken before initiation into the deeper mysteries are symbols widespread throughout the world. North American Indians usually go into a sweat lodge where they sit in a chamber under the earth; water is poured over the hot stones so that the man sits in hot steam while rubbing himself with sage grass as a means of cleansing himself from the sins he has committed and from the evil spirits.

In early interpretations, Christian baptism is also understood as a cleansing and separation from sin and the chasing away of evil spirits. There is a connection here with the idea of renewal, for the person who was baptised was renewed in Christ and had put off former pagan sins. As proof of this a white garment was worn, indicative of purification and of the new personality. The same implication is to be found in most of the different ritual baths, together with the idea of renewal by water.

In general, water refers to the unconscious and going into the water and coming out again seems to have a certain analogy with going into the unconscious. The baptismal font in Christianity is frequently compared with the uterus of the Mother Church and has therefore a maternal aspect—one is reborn in the eternal womb, which is the water. It is the maternal place from which one came and to which one returns in a new form. In early times only grown-up people were baptised and were completely immersed. Infant baptism came about through the belief that only the baptised would go to Heaven and see God, and naturally Christian parents did not want their children to die as heathens. In the Dead Sea Scrolls, there is also mention of renewal by baptism.

In many dreams the analytical process is likened to taking a bath and analysis is often compared with washing or bathing. In German you talk of "washing someone's head," i.e., scolding them, or showing them where they are wrong in their ideas. Most people when they come to analysis have an awkward feeling that something of the kind is necessary and that their sins might come out. Thus the idea of a bath is a very obvious simile. The dirt which covers the body might mean psychological influences in the surroundings which have contaminated the original personality.

It is much easier to be oneself and natural if one lives alone. Introverts are very sensitive and often say that they are all right when alone but that with other people they pick up disturbing influences and lose their inner serenity. All patients are not ambitious, but if one patient makes a move to do something the others all want to do the same. That is the phenomenon of mass psychology, and here primitive emotions prevail. Reason is wiped out by infection and less educated people con-

taminate others and all are pulled down. If one has the same
potentiality, that is immediately activated. As soon as you
enter the human herd you deteriorate and your own shadow is
constellated. You can say that your own darkness is activated
from outside, but one can also really pick up darkness which
is not one's own. People get lured into attitudes which are not
theirs, and when they have time to think they wonder what
happened to them. That is something which we have to clean
up again and again and so we generally interpret the bath as
the need to work through shadow problems.

There is a great temptation to apply this meaning to fairytales and say that the anima figure has to go through the process of renewal, but if we do so we forget our own hypothesis,
namely that the figures are archetypal and not human. So we
can say that the bath, the water, is a return to the unconscious
in order to be cleansed from certain shadow aspects which do
not really belong. If the anima has to go through the process
it is not the same thing as if the human being has to do so. The
neurotic complex is faced, not the human being; it is pushed
back into the water, i.e., into the unconscious, where the neurotic destructive impulses are dealt with by the method of
amplification. One has to look at the dreams and see what lies
behind. When you amplify a dream you put it back into its
original context. The dream fragment is dipped into the
amniotic fluid so that it gets enriched and through this enlarging process can appear again in a different form.

The bath has to do with amplification, or with the psychological attitude of restoring the complex to its original fullness
and seeing what kind of forces are working in it. Neurotic
symptoms are often the result of something having become
stuck between the unconscious and consciousness. I will give
you an example. A girl had a complex which imprisoned her in
her flat. As soon as she was in the street, or in a tram, her complex told her that any labourer she met would infect her with

25

syphilis; though she knew quite well that this was an impossibility, she could not be reasonable and could not argue the idea away.

Obviously the girl funked work, for the labourer represents the working energy. Through funking work her working energy became negative and disturbed her erotic functions. The disease came through her father complex. Over and over again she had started to work, but then left off and her father, who was a wealthy man, always gave in to her. Therefore the labourer in working clothes infected her—the energy which was not used infected the personality in a destructive form, especially attacking the woman where she was most vulnerable, i.e., in her femininity. Eros and love are contaminated and destroyed by the unused energy libido. The unconscious clearly gave her a healing message, but she had not understood it. Dr. Jung gave only half an hour to the symptom and the patient was cured in that half hour. There was a strong ethical integrity in her and she swallowed the pill and began to work. He told her that she would land in an asylum if she did not.

Here you see that the girl appears to be imprisoned in something completely destructive, but in the symbolism of the symptom the unconscious has shown the cure. Healing messages do sometimes work destructively if not understood and used rightly. They remain on the threshold of consciousness. A symbolic message of the unconscious is like a cursed being, a content which got stuck in an in-between sphere because of conditions in the unconscious which did not allow it to come up; if you push it back and then let it come up in its full original meaning, the destructive effect goes.

Let us examine the motif of the princess being beaten with hazel sticks. The hazel tree and its branches, especially in Celtic and Germanic mythology, have to do with the wisdom of truthfulness—the wise salmon who has eaten the hazel nuts found growing round the water can advise the heroes. The hazel stick has to do with impersonal truthfulness and objectivity. In the old Germanic Thing (a meeting of the free men of the tribe), when one of their members had to be judged, before the trial started they would take a peeled hazel stick, a symbol by which they owned to not being subjectively honest, while at the same time outwardly expressing their intention of being as objective and honest as possible in their judgement. This reminds one of the royal sceptre, which also represents an impersonal principle of authority, not a personal power complex. Therefore, if the hero beats the princess with a hazel stick he gives her an unpleasant truth in an objective way, just as the interpretation of a dream gives an objective truth, and this has an exorcising effect.

The meaning of a dream may be very painful and cut like a whip, it may say that a hated person is like oneself, but the impersonal, objective criticism is cleansed of its destructive aspect. That the hazel stick is something naturally grown is also very meaningful. God allows some people to be lazy and one should not be so arrogant as to presume to know exactly how people should behave; some people may do the most amazing things without punishment. Laziness in some civilizations is quite normal and such people are not neurotic. But if a symptom appears, then that is another thing, for it has grown in the soul of the patient.

Total repression of a complex could be compared to the shutting up of the whole thing in a lead coffin, whereas the death of a complex might be illustrated by the transfer of the libido (psychic energy), as for instance in the following case.

A peasant girl practised black magic and often dreamt of her grandfather who during his lifetime had held séances, but whom she had never seen. In one dream he appeared as a hermaphrodite, half man and half woman. In the unconscious the hermaphrodite symbolises "this and also that." It illustrates the in-between or "stuck" nature of the complex. Here there were two things involved: an unsatisfied, undeveloped mind on the one hand, and on the other a very passionate feminine

27

nature which she repressed. The two had formed a hermaphroditic monster. She had to sort this out in analysis. She had a
dream in which she had to go down into her mother's bedroom,
deep in a cave, where a wonderful woman gave birth to a child,
a miraculous birth brought about by an angel. At the same time,
she heard moaning, and saw that the grandfather was in bed
dying. Thus, as soon as the feminine personality was born in
her soul, the monster lost its energy and the black magic of the
grandfather was shed like an empty shell and with this her interest in it faded. She realized that it had been an impotent
attempt to get what she wanted. The libido hitherto in the
black magic went over to the psychic process of individuation.

Usually baths are not taken in the sea but in a bathtub,
which gives a very definite nuance, since a bathtub is a man-
made vessel into which the human being can enter, and it is of
a definite size. It represents the unconscious in a very specific
form so we have to go into the symbolism of the vessel, which
is tremendous. The vessel is the womb of the Mother Church,
the uterus, and so it has a definite feminine maternal quality.
It is mythologically often contaminated with its content. For
the alchemist, the vessel and the water are the same thing. The
water is the vessel in which the philosopher's stone is made,
for the container and the content in alchemy are brought completely together. Since the vessel is a man-made means of keeping water, it has to do with the function of consciousness; to
be able to use the instrument is a prerogative of human consciousness and points to its activities as a symbol. The vessel
would represent a concept, or a way of conceiving of a thing.

The Church is such a vessel for it provides a way by which
the Christian religious values and ideas are held together by a
dogmatic system. Psychologically, the vessel has to do with
vows, ideas, basic feelings, and concepts which we try to hold
together and keep from escaping in life, for the vessel can hold
these things so that they are not lost. It therefore constitutes
a means of becoming conscious.

In many languages conception and understanding express the function of the container—a means of grasping and catching in a certain form, the idea or thing being bent into a shape in which it can be handled. The alchemist's technique was not to have here a system and here a phenomenon of the psyche, but to have a psychological concept of the psyche derived from itself. This is easily forgotten. We have learnt the Jungian system with concepts such as animus and anima, but therein lies a danger. Actually, Dr. Jung derived his concepts from his own experience of the unconscious, so that here vessel and content are the same thing. We try to understand the psyche by means of the psyche, and this is called "symbolic thinking." We do not conceive of a compulsive neurosis as being composed of such and such phenomena to be cured in such and such a way.

The idea is that we should see how the psyche deals with the problem—that is the secret identity of the content and the container. The alchemists thought that matter could teach them how to deal with matter. Nevertheless, we have a certain amount of method, e.g., dream interpretation, and certain views on the nature of the psyche and this general attitude can be compared to the symbol of the vessel. In contrast to the Freudians, we do not encourage the patient to let loose an endless stream of associations, but stick to the symbol and the motif so that it shall not be dissolved in the whole sea of the unconscious. We draw an elastic borderline between what belongs and what does not.

To know what belongs is a question of practical skill. If there is a semi-conscious complex, as for instance in the case of the girl with the syphilis complex, we push it back into the water of the bathtub without letting it leak all over the place—childish reminiscences would not belong here. We keep within a certain field and try to feel the way by the emotion of the patient. There is thus enough of the unknown, so that the complex can manifest itself, for otherwise one would be lost in the infinity of the unconscious. Then coming afterwards is

29

the stewing, or bathing in hot water, the cool bath, the hot bath, and the fire bath. The symbolism of temperature naturally refers to emotional intensity; what arouses one's emotion is hot. Coolness is associated with pacifying; it is less emotional or it may even be a wet blanket which is put over the enthusiasm. Water also represents a kind of emotion, the waves of the sea being the movement of the water. Generally this is not mentioned. Coolness might have to do with reason.

You may want to convince the analysand that in this particular situation nothing can be decided but that what is going on should be understood. The worst passion comes when people are faced with an unknown factor. Panic is destructive. It is an aimless excitement like that of a panicky animal. Panic outbursts are often represented in psychoses as the conflagration of the world, or a married man may fall in love with another woman and get into a panic as to what must be done. The sudden excitement of not being able to cope with the situation is the dangerous conflagration of the personality. Here understanding is the quieting instrument. One endeavours to lead the person to the wider concept and to show that the conflict is brought about by one's own soul and not by oneself. If realization of what is aimed at can be reached, even though it may be without understanding, and the decision is made to do nothing at the time, the danger of panic goes and is succeeded by a waiting attitude. Then a reasonable human solution may be expected instead of the panic of destruction. Man is most dangerous when the fire of passion has taken possession of him. The water in the bath has very much to do with the penetration of understanding.

In Jung's essay "The Psychology of the Transference," there are some interesting passages on water and the bath where the understanding quality of the water symbol is shown in a great deal of material and compared with the water of wisdom of the alchemists. Here there is mention also of the necessity of having intellectual understanding and a feeling relation to the contents of the unconscious.*

I had a case of a woman in a deadly panic. She wanted to commit suicide at once and the psychiatrist with whom I was working wanted to intern her. I asked her for her dreams and she said that she had had a vision in which she saw an egg and heard a voice which said "the mother and daughter." I amplified this material, saying that the egg was the germ of the new possibility, and so on. She was so far gone that she did not understand a word of explanation and said afterwards that she had not been able to listen, but after I had talked for a while she quietened and said she would go home. I therefore suggested that she should not be interned. Later she explained that though she had not understood what I said, she thought that Fraulein von Franz had considered the dream to be positive.

The fact that someone understands is enough, even though one cannot understand oneself—then the temperature drops and a certain quietness comes, and then perhaps the patient may also understand. Archetypal contents are sometimes far away and if the patient is not drawn to them in these terms you cannot get the meaning across, but the feeling that somebody else understands has a calming effect.

*Collected Works, Vol. 16, pars. 453ff and 483ff.

Lecture 3

Last time we discussed the motif of the cooling effect of the bath. The Catholic Church speaks of the *aqua doctrinae,* the water of the doctrine, the water symbolising the quieting effect brought to the soul by the dogma. When there is a possibility of understanding, emotion is cooled and quietened. In the fairytale the redeeming bath is frequently very hot and only the hero is capable of withstanding a temperature in which others would perish. In one version the old king endeavours to destroy the hero in a bath, but the latter's horse is endowed with magic qualities and can cool the water with his breath and the hero comes out unharmed. He then invites the king to get into the bath and he is boiled to death. Here it is a question not of the cleansing effect of the water, but of the secret magic of the hero which preserves him from being boiled in the bath or cooked in the stove.

Hot water would stand for emotion: when we work on a complex by pushing it back into the unconscious, we add libido by participating emotionally with whatever comes up. Often the complex itself has a certain affect quality and in such a case we can cook it in its own affect. It is possible for the hot water, or emotion, to come out together with a projection and then the whole emotion flows towards the outer object. An analysand may have a shadow which he tries to abreact by getting into a rage with another person, but this has to be shown up as a projection so that the analysand or complex has to stew in its own juice; for when the normal outlet of projection is closed, then the agony begins, and since it is no longer possible to make the outer world the scapegoat one is forced

32

to suffer oneself from the impact of the complex, which has no other exit.

The analysand may have negative affects against the analyst and if the latter reacts emotionally, an issue is provided, whereas if he keeps outside it the emotion is shut off into the analysand himself who has to suffer it. This method is not always the right one for sometimes one must enter into the emotional play, but this is a question of the correct interpretation of the dreams and of adopting the corresponding attitude and knowing when emotion must be kept inside the analysand, who is then in a hot bath with the complex, which always involves tremendous suffering.

Actually, this is a picture of Hell where you boil in hot oil and have to stay in it. This happens to people daily when they sit and boil in their own emotional complexes. Even people who do not believe in Hell are struck by this image which expresses a certain psychological truth.

Heating the bath from outside would imply that the emotion is artificially intensified. This one can see chiefly in schizoid cases when people may have tremendous problems without suffering adequately from them. The affect does not appear where one might expect it, but bursts out somewhere else. Dr. Jung speaks of a patient who when asked what it was that he wrote down during an interview, replied that he wrote when he telephoned the Virgin Mary. If a normal person had a vision of, or a conversation with, the Virgin Mary, he would be overawed, but a schizophrenic can talk in the same breath of any everyday thing, such as his cigarettes, for instance. In such a case, or in borderline cases, the bath has to be heated artificially, which means that the psychotherapy has to add the emotion which is lacking. For instance, a schizophrenic patient may threaten to shoot the analyst without in the least realizing what he is saying, and then one has to produce an affect to give him a shock and produce the normal reaction. If there is a possibility of saving such a case it is through mak-

33

ing the analysand realize what he says, that is, by heating the bath from the outside and adding the emotion which has not been adequately produced internally.

In schizophrenia the unconscious contents have a tendency to disintegrate, thus losing their normal emotional value. In a neurosis, the neurotic shut-off part of the personality will have its adequate emotional life, while in a psychotic case the tendency to disintegrate more and more without emotional affect is the difficulty. Such people can be hurt by a remark you may make, without realizing that they have been hurt, but they have an affect later. I once made a remark which hit an analysand's complex, but he went away quite happy. About an hour later, in the street, he suddenly had the idea that a man in a truck intended to shoot him and a tremendous rage welled up in him— the reaction was in a completely inappropriate place. I remarked that something must have hurt him in the interview, since a dream had pointed in that direction, but he did not remember anything—the part which I had hit was so shut off that he had not noticed anything. Actually he had dreamt that somebody had been killed and thrown into a hole in the ground and that then the corpse itself had disappeared, leaving nothing but a bit of the clothing. In this way the complex becomes an autonomous content which disintegrates.

It is well known in analysis that someone who has been hurt may dream of somebody being killed, but the schizoid analysand who has not realized anything has the tremendous rage against the man on the truck; one cannot find the association without a great deal of trouble, and it is practically impossible to reconstruct the situation as to what happened underneath. Therefore, in cases where the complex is not expressed with adequate emotion it must be given outside libido to prevent it from disintegrating, so that it may become strong enough to well up in its right form—one has then concentrated attention on the problem. A problem may be repressed and shut up in a drawer for years and years and the person may refuse to look

34

at it, saying that if he did so he might get into a depression. That would be refusing to give the shut-off part of the personality the necessary attention in order to escape the suffering of the boiling bath.

The *Benedictio Fontis,* baptism in the Church, represents the cleansing of the human being and his transformation into a new spiritual being; but the symbolism in the Mass has been tremendously elaborated, whereas in fairytales we find the natural process. On the Saturday before Easter the baptismal water is always blessed. The priest divides the water into four parts by making the sign of the cross over it, i.e., the blood of Christ has streamed from the four-armed cross over the whole world and towards a new paradise, and the water becomes an instrument for the rebirth of souls. Thus it is said that the Holy Ghost will impregnate the water prepared for the rebirth of man with the mysterious admixture of the divine power, so that out of this uterus of the divine font a new creature may be born and a divine generation come up. Those who have been separated by sin and old age are all reborn to the same childhood through the Mother Church and the grace of God, and every impure spirit flees away and may not approach the water. The purified human is thus revivified and absolved from sin and then blessed three times with the sign of the cross. Here the aspects of cleansing and giving rebirth are united. The priest holds the Easter candle in the water and blesses it three times in the form of the + cross. The light and rebirth quality of the Holy Ghost enters the water at that moment and it is said that the Holy Ghost enters the baptismal water so that those who are baptised are really reborn.

The gesture of the fire of the Easter candle entering the water is psychological. We might say that the light of the candle would represent the light of an understanding attitude, an enlightenment of the mind which now enters the unconscious and fertilizes it. That would represent an attitude of voluntary sacrifice, a certain conscious understanding and knowledge of the truth obtained by dipping it in the water, i.e., handing it back to the unconscious from whence it came so that it may be increased in power and effect. There is also the union of the opposites—the fire and water—and the result is a fiery water. The baptismal water of the Church is often called *aqua ignita* since it is said to contain the fire of the Holy Ghost and expresses the total reality of the truth, the union of the conscious and unconscious attitudes. If you wish to interpret this more in the ideas of the Church, you can add that it is always said that every truth of the Catholic Church contains a mystery and can only be interpreted to a point; there is always something which cannot be explained in dogmatic formulas and representations. The light of the candle would represent that aspect of the Church which is unknown, reunited with another aspect. By the symbolic quality, the unconscious as well as the conscious mind of the participant is touched, giving the truth a double quality. It is a symbol of renewal of the attitude.

People who have had a long analysis do not need such a complete analysis of a dream as in the beginning; an allusion suffices, which would be a parallel to aspersion by the sprinkling of the holy water (the *asperges*). This replaces immersion in the bath which is aesthetically an unpleasant procedure.

During the holidays I saw a film showing the baptismal rites of the Mandeans (a people who live in the territory situated between the Tigris and the Euphrates) where there is a ritual in which all household objects have to be immersed in a large bath. It is very difficult not to see the unaesthetic and amusing aspect when, for instance, the billy goat is pushed into the water and everybody gets covered with mud and water. As you know, the development in the Catholic Church has been to eliminate such things for more differentiated aspects, but, on the other hand, if you see the primitive bath you are impressed by the original life of such a performance. The people meet secretly in the night and read from their sacred book. A

36

hole is dug and everybody is bathed, as well as all household utensils, and afterwards there is a ritualistic meal. Though it is not aesthetic and one cannot help laughing at some aspects, it does represent the original emotion once contained in the ceremony much better than more elaborate rituals.

We should not forget that immersion in a bath is a definite somatic experience. After a long period spent in a hut on the mountains it is refreshing and wonderful to have a bath which has an immediate revivifying effect, such as one does not experience in a daily bath. In psychiatry, the bath is used to help in the lighter catatonic states and depressions, since massage and bathing have a revivifying effect on the body and the circulation of the blood.

We now go on to the motif of eating flowers, another strange fairytale motif. In Apuleius's story *The Golden Ass,* the hero is turned into an ass and can only be redeemed by eating roses. The novelist has taken this motif out of folklore. The theme of the human being who is turned into an animal and can only be redeemed by eating flowers appears all over the world. The flowers may be lilies, not necessarily roses, depending on the country in which the story is told. A simple German story relates that a man woos the beautiful daughter of a witch and goes away to the war. Mother and daughter decide that he has been unfaithful and on his return they transform him into an ass. He is obliged to carry the miller's sacks for a long time, until one day, while he is passing the witch's house, he overhears the daughter ask her mother whether they should not turn him back into a human, and he learns that if he eats lilies he will become human again. He does so and is transformed. He then stands naked before the people and explains what has happened. This is the original, simple version upon which Apuleius's story is based.

First we must discuss what it means for a human being to be turned into an animal. Different animals have different instinctive behaviour; if a tiger behaved like a squirrel, we would

37

call it neurotic. For a human being to be turned into an animal is for him to be out of his own instinctive sphere, estranged from it, and one must look at the specific animal in question. Take the ass: this is one of the animals of the god Dionysus. It was known in antiquity as being very sexual and is also known for its perseverance and so-called stupidity. It is one of Saturn's animals and has the Saturnine qualities. Saturn in late antiquity was regarded as the god of the Jews, and in disputes between Christians and non-Christians, both Christians and Jews were accused of worshipping the ass. Therefore to be turned into an ass would imply being overwhelmed by such qualities, i.e., to have fallen under the drive of a specific complex which imposed such behaviour. In Apuleius's story it is obviously the sexual drive which is in the foreground. The man has enjoyed a sexual affair with a kitchenmaid and got drowned in sensual pleasure. Then there is the aspect of melancholia associated with Saturn.

Depressions and melancholy are often a cover for tremendous greed. At the beginning of an analysis there is often a depressed state of resignation—life has no meaning, there is no feeling of being in life. An exaggerated state can develop into complete lameness. Quite young people give the impression of having the resignation of a bitter old man or woman. When you dig into such a black mood you find that behind it there is overwhelming greed—for being loved, for being very rich, for having the right partner, for being the top dog, etc. Behind such a melancholic resignation you will often discover in the darkness a recurring theme which makes things very difficult, namely if you give such people one bit of hope, the lion opens its mouth and you have to withdraw, and then they put the lid on again, and so it goes on, back and forth. It is either all or nothing. People swing between resigned depression on one side and the bringing out of enormous claims on the other. This is typical of the *nigredo* of the alchemists, with the symbols of black mists and ravens flying about and, the alchemists

38

say, "all wild animals walking past." Also in the traditional stage from the *nigredo* to the *albedo* you have the transition of all wild animals coming up, one group after the other: sex, power, infantile drives, etc.

Thus to be turned into an animal is not to live according to one's own instincts, but to be partially overwhelmed by a one-sided instinctive drive which upsets the human balance. Now it becomes more difficult if, as often happens in a fairytale, a person not the hero, say the anima, is the figure which is turned into an animal and has to be redeemed by the hero. In the Grimm fairytale "The Golden Bird," the hero is always accompanied and helped by a fox who gives the right advice and help. After the happy marriage of the hero with the princess, the fox appears one day and asks to be beheaded and to have his paws cut off. The hero refuses. The fox retires, but then reappears and asks again. With a deep sigh the hero complies and the fox becomes a beautiful prince who proves to be the brother of the princess and now redeemed.

If you dreamt that not you yourself but another figure had been turned into an animal, the hypothesis would be that the ego complex had been overwhelmed by another complex. Let us assume that a man dreams that a woman he loves, his anima figure, is turned into a black dog; that is, the anima, which should have a human field of experience, a human expression (the inner life which has reached a human level), has been overwhelmed by a drive, has regressed into a pre-human form of expression through the influence of inner complexes.

The anima would be personified by a human being, and all the man's anima reactions—moods and emotions, the form and tone through which he attracts other women—at first are on the level of a human woman. But then a witch or wizard curses the anima, transforming her into a black dog, which would mean that another completely unconscious complex has contaminated the anima with its content, exercising a destructive and damaging influence on her. In the realm of the fringe of

39

consciousness you can do nothing until the ego can interfere, therefore a cursed animal needs the help of the hero to get out of its state, i.e., it cannot free itself. In European fairytales, the wizard generally represents the dark aspect of the image of God which has not been recognized in collective consciousness. The wizard has all the characteristics of a dark pagan god, perhaps Wotan, or a troll, or a mountain demon, or some other Celtic pre-Christian image of God. Therefore it can be said that such gods represent an aspect of the image of God which has not been consciously accepted and so has lived a dark life; it has an unconscious *Weltanschauung*, a point of view or philosophy of life, which influences the anima. A man's anima often has a *Weltanschauung,* and that is difficult for men to understand.

A man can describe his own anima quite well and knows his own anima reactions, but what is complicated is that such an anima is not only an expression of moods and feelings, but that she carries the *Weltanschauung* and has ethical standards. If his anima is attracted to beautiful, uninhibited women or young girls, then he will understand that his feeling life has the quality of looking at life in a naive way and is not as inhibited as his conscious mind, but the worst thing is that if he tries to get near the complex of the young anima that will impose on him the problem of *Weltanschauung,* which can challenge his conscious attitude. If a man discovers that his anima always wants him to seduce young girls, then the anima is not only the expression of a mood but tends towards deeds and thoughts which are in contradiction to the *Weltanschauung* of the man and occasion a tremendous problem. He can accept the love of beauty and young life, but cannot accept what he has to do if he follows her.

So the anima is the carrier of a different *Weltanschauung.* In our society she is often a pagan; she loves the beauty of life, the beauty of nature in its beyond good and evil form, and that is her *Weltanschauung,* and that is the peculiar problem. She challenges the whole conscious attitude of the man. The real trouble is that his anima has been influenced by another complex, and he must first deal with the wizard and its negative influences and say: "I have one *Weltanschauung* and my soul has another." Since the problem of the *Weltanschauung* is much more serious to the man than the problem of feeling, that is where men have their greatest difficulty.

The assumption that there is another complex behind the anima is proved by the fact that in dreams the anima often appears as having another lover and then the man has dreams of jealousy. This is a kind of representation from the unconscious that the anima is tied to another complex in the unconscious, and which is the anima and which the other complex has to be sorted out.

Take the example of a man who in his conscious life is not ambitious but is a lazy, peaceful type of man who does not want to overwork, but he has an ambitious shadow who is not seen by him consciously and through whom he always falls for women who promise to make him a great man. Because of his unconscious ambition he always falls for those women who have the famous man-catching trick of promising to be an inspiring anima to give him the wings with which to fly to the top. Such a man may dream that his anima went off with a very ambitious and disagreeable fellow. His anima has been contaminated by his ambition. As soon as he realizes his ambition he no longer falls for such women. That was his unconscious ambition and that he could face. But if the anima has a *Weltanschauung,* it is because she is contaminated with one of the male complexes. The anima in a man is an impulse towards life, or out of life. She entangles him in life and disentangles him from it, but she has no definite *Weltanschauung*, or if she has, it is a paradoxical one—yes and no. A *Weltanschauung* here is a tendency in the unconscious which cannot get into consciousness and therefore takes hold of the anima instead. It always implies one complex behind another, so it

41

is more direct to talk of the *Weltanschauung* of the anima. That is represented as her unfaithfulness: she goes off with another man—an unconscious characteristic of his own—without his noticing it. Then comes the problem that the anima has to be freed from the destructive influence and the wizard killed.

In European fairytales, the anima is in the clutches of the devil and then the hero and the anima have to run away from him until they are safe—he has to get his anima away from the devilish influence of the unconscious.

The next question is why does the wizard throw the animal skin over the anima? When he curses her, this is what he does, and then you meet a black dog instead of a beautiful lady. Underneath the animal skin is a suffering human being, but when you go into the unconscious you may first meet a black dog.

In the story of the ass, the witch throws the skin over the hero himself. You can bewitch people by running and throwing a skin over them. In Grimm's "The Six Swans," the sister has to make shirts which have to be finished by a certain time and these have to be thrown over the brothers who then become human again. But as one sleeve is not finished the youngest brother keeps one wing. Thus a being can be redeemed or cursed by a skin being thrown over it. To throw the skin over someone is another way of applying the curse. Practically, this means that a complex of the psyche which has human means of expression is so depotentiated that it has only animal means of expression. There is always a reason, but sometimes it is direct and sometimes indirect.

There is often such a "drivenness" connected with a complex that one is robbed of expression. You may know exactly what you want to say about a problem when you are alone, you are quite clear about it, but as soon as you get into the situation you are overwhelmed by emotion and can only

42

stammer, or make a sign; you are prevented from human expression. If you quarrel with someone, the moment you start to talk you cannot say a word because your ethical conscious stops you and you literally behave like an ass and can only say "hee-haw." This leads to the famous letter writing, for as soon as the analysand is home he realizes what he wanted to say, but in the hour he could only say "hee-haw," or he became stupid and could only behave awkwardly or say things in a confused way. This is the stupefying effect of emotion.

In such a case what is potentially human within one is, by the interference of another complex, pushed back into the emotions, the animal-like state of expression. This is generally directly or indirectly caused by a prejudice in the conscious ego attitude, a wrong attitude in the ego which gives the person no chance of expressing himself adequately. It has not an open ear for what the anima might have to say. Such men may say of the anima: "It is nothing but sexuality."

If you think of the anima as being "nothing but" what you know about her, you have not the receptiveness of a listening attitude, and so she becomes "nothing but" a load of brutal emotions; you have never given her a chance of expressing herself, and therefore she has become inhuman and brutal. This is why Dr. Jung introduced active imagination, as a means of talking to the complex: you ask the black dog into your room and talk to him, listening carefully to what he says. You will see then that the overload disappears and is replaced by a relatively human being with whom you can talk and you find out that it is the wizard. The human being has hitherto rejected the anima and the wizard has taken it out on her. It is like killing the wife or the child to hurt the other person. You can say in such a case that the ego has somewhere blocked one complex by another; then one is bewitched as an act of vengeance. If it is a pagan *Weltanschauung* which is behind the anima, the man would have to ask and ascertain his own stand-

43

point: "Why do such ideas exist in my soul?" The influence on his anima will then stop and he will see that she is harmless in herself.

I recall a man who was consciously very rational who had had a great shock in his early youth, at the age of puberty. His mother had died of cancer in a slow and horrible way, and as a young boy he had had to watch his beloved mother dying slowly before his eyes. From being very lively and temperamental, he became silent and dried up and developed a resemblance to his very rational father, with all his belief in life gone. What he did not realize, but which came out in the analysis in dreams and visions, was that he unconsciously drew the conclusion that there was no good God: if such a wonderful being as his mother could be innocently tortured to death by such a terrible illness, then God was responsible for this. He was not enough of a religious philosopher to make such a reflection, but he drew the conclusion unconsciously and from that time on this idea governed his life—i.e., "I know that anyhow the world is wicked and life evil"—but his conscious attitude was one of rational scepticism.

The first appearance in his dreams was a tremendously vital anima which showed the exuberance of an antique Venus. He was bothered by sexual fantasies of a normal nature—e.g., a woman would appear at his bedside, exciting him, or he would dream of Dionysian dinner parties. In reality he was rather an ascetic person who did not enjoy life at all; at a party everybody avoided him, but he had an anima with pagan experience and sensation. I pushed him to follow up this anima, saying that if he saw a girl who responded to the picture he should do something about it. That worked for a time and then not any more. Was it a neurotic mechanism which stopped him, or was it something else? I followed the indications of the dreams, sometimes telling him to telephone the girl, and sometimes not to do so.

Once at the end of a semester he came with the following

44

dream: A beautiful naked woman with a marvellous figure approached his bed with signs and gestures, exciting him sexually, but disappeared when he tried to catch hold of her. Then this same beautiful woman came down a staircase carrying, like Moses, a tablet in her hand, on which appeared the words: "You can't have me." I was so discouraged and perplexed that I said: "Yes, that is how it is." But afterwards he realized for the first time what the anima was! The next time he came he said: "Last time you accomplished a miracle! Now I understand what the anima is!" My own reflection was that I had not been aware of having accomplished anything, but he had realized the paradoxical nature of the anima. He also realized that it was up to him, that he had to make the decision and take the problem in hand, and he suddenly realized that he had to do something. He said: "To Hell with this anima with her double play, I am going to work and will paint!"

All his pictures and inner visions showed a dark, devilish, divine figure attacking him—the dark god—and he realized that this was the real cause of his depression. He had always wanted everything, had indulged in childish hopes of finding the beautiful woman, and then dropped back into resignation. His depression was like that of a frustrated baby. Now he suddenly saw that behind it was his pessimistic *Weltanschauung,* that he did not believe in life or God and that he must work out his image of God. His mother's terrible illness had touched her brain; he saw how affected she had been and from her sufferings he had drawn the unconscious conclusion that there was no psyche. His whole *Weltanschauung* had to be discussed at great length, for his anima had been depreciated into a low type of woman who was also wicked, her wickedness being caused by the other block, for the anima is generally a morally indifferent being. Though she had reached the conscious level, his only approach to her was in a very primitive form, that of a crude sexual attack, that is, like an animal. Behind this he had very human feelings but he had not developed any way of

45

expressing them. Even though he might love a woman he knew no other way of expressing his feeling; his anima was bewitched in this way for he was dominated by his materialistic ideas.

If you believe that sex is only a question of the hormones in the body, then sex becomes a mechanical thing, just like driving a car, without any meaning of a psychological feeling relationship. This man was punished for his wrong idea by temporary impotence, his body saying: "If you think I am only a car, then the car won't function any more!" The wrong conscious attitude had produced psychogenic impotence. Consciously, his attitude was that if you behaved properly you were entitled to human happiness, but his mother had been happy and well behaved and had been destroyed in a sadistic manner, for that was how he had experienced her death. Yet, consciously, he still thought that God was good and that life owed him happiness. He could not understand why he did not get what he wanted, so he came to the conclusion that things were different *for him. He* was the one who had nothing and he had decided to put up with this and to give up trying to get anything out of life; the leaden lid of resignation came over him and with it a tremendous bitterness, and his legitimate claim to feeling was suppressed. He had never faced up to what he really thought. He was not a thinking type and was resigned to the idea that life was like that. He even felt guilty, believing that he must be an awful person since his fate was so bad. Thus he had to realize that God had a dark side.

One has to consider what effect it would have on one to have to accept the fact that God was not the friendly guardian of a kindergarten! Even the Christian dogma says that God has an incomprehensible side, and if you can realize this then you can grow away from the idea that if you are well behaved then you will be happy. This man got out of his infantile mechanism, becoming more earnest and sad consciously, but less bitter and melancholic. Through realization of the dark image he acquired a certain wisdom. Hitherto also he had been very

46

critical of human reactions, but through the realization of the dark side of God, and the precarious situation of man, he became more tolerant and understanding, realizing that we are all poor devils struggling with a difficult fate, the beginning and end of which we do not know. He thus began to accept the small happinesses of life, which you can enjoy much more if you know that life is difficult and dark, and he acquired a certain sense of humour which he had not formerly possessed.

In his case one could have said: "The fear of God is the beginning of wisdom." He got something relatively equivalent to his dream because he could see something of the beauty of life and its meaningfulness in a much more humble way, since he had lost his infantile greed and the idea that something was owed to him. One of his own shadow figures was a gangster, and if you believe that everything in life is negative, then the gangster's idea of life is the right one! Thus being consciously very correct, he always dreamt of the gangster-shadow, for if life was so rotten then one should take a pistol and grab! He had another shadow who was a very sensuous man who lived just to eat and drink. This was the figure who liked to make such friends in outer life. He had a friend who was a great drinker and a coarse eater and who had the same *Weltanschauung* as himself. All his unconscious complexes were influenced by the image induced by the shock he had sustained and which had produced the images of the gangster and the materialistic drinker, as well as his resentful attitude towards cripples, for he projected onto others that thing which was crippled in his own soul.

Lecture 4

Last time we discussed what it would mean if a content of the collective unconscious were transformed into an animal, and we got stuck in the discussion because in our story we have first to find out why the figure of the anima is transformed, or bewitched, by the figure of the devilish old man. I tried to explain that the anima can be under the influence of an unconscious *Weltanschauung*, or point of view, and that this influence, which emanates from the man's soul, can affect the other complexes. This would presuppose that the complexes of the human psyche are not just a cluster of particles but that they have a kind of social organization among themselves, that they influence or dominate each other, and that their centralization is due to the archetype of the Self. If this is true, then it is conceivable that one influences the other, dominates the other, and that complexes can also melt into each other.

Through the story which we have taken, we have shown what it would mean if a wizard cursed a princess, making her behave in an evil way. In the case in question the anima had been cursed by a Nordic nature spirit (a troll) which lives in a mountain (other trolls live in the sea).

We have still not explained the motif of the animal skin, but first I want to bring to your attention some theoretical reflections by Dr. Jung regarding the psyche. These are taken from his essay entitled "On the Nature of the Psyche."*

Jung here tries to give a description of what we would like to call the psyche and compares it to the scale of the colours, the spectrum with its two poles, the infra-red and ultra-

*Collected Works, Vol. 8, pars. 414ff.

violet. He says that, naturally, it would be possible to say that everything is the psyche, but that he prefers to presume that there is such a phenomenon as matter which we do *not* call the psyche, for though it is related, we do not quite know how. This would provide a subject for study by physicists, it would be non-psychic. Another concept is the spirit, which can be defined as that element which appears in the psyche as a manifestation of order, and which might also appear in matter in the same way.

Wherever we have the phenomenon of a meaningful order, we assume it to be the work of this spirit. We cannot prove that there is such a thing as spirit, we simply define it by that unknown element which creates order. Neither matter nor spirit can be observed and described directly. As you know, matter is identical with energy, and both are an "X" for the physicist, who can describe the behaviour of matter, but cannot define what it is in itself. The same is true for the spirit, but we can observe in the psyche an activity which creates order and therefore assume that something is the source of this activity; that something is what we call spirit. Matter in the human being would then be the body, and the spirit aspect of the human being would be the sum of the archetypes, because the archetypes, according to our view, are those unknown elements which manifest as creating order in the psychic realm.

Please do not confuse an archetype with an image or symbol; the archetype is the unknown factor which produces the archetypal image. What makes the image is only an assumed reality. We assume there is such a thing since something must make that image, but we cannot demonstrate it as an entity in itself. The basic structure which creates the images is what we call the ordering spirit or archetypes.

If we observe the behaviour of an animal we can only describe it from outside. In a book on zoology you can read that bees build their cells in a certain way, their queen behaves in such and such a way, and so on. The physical activity of the

49

insect or animal and its pattern of behaviour is described, but if we presume that such behaviour is meaningful for the bees, then we have projected something onto them. We can only say that this is the way they appear to behave, and so far we have had no means of seeing how the thing looks from the point of view of the animal. We do not know what kind of emotion the queen bee has when producing her eggs. We can assume a great deal, but cannot scientifically observe it.

If we watch the higher animals it seems likely that they have feelings similar to our own. I have discussed this with Konrad Lorenz and he says he is convinced this is so, but that he cannot prove it. Anybody who has had a dog or one of the higher animals for a while, believes that when they are carrying out any of their instinctual patterns of behaviour they experience feelings comparable to our own. For instance, my own dog, when a puppy, would go through the gestures of making a hole, putting a bone into it, and scratching non-existent earth over it. Having done this, he would race up and down the room a few times exhibiting pleasure. He had again performed something on his instinctual pattern and I can only say that it seemed to me that he got a kick out of it, but this cannot be proved. How much does a dog visualize or image? It can imagine puppies! The human being also can be accurately described and his physical behaviour photographed.

Lorenz constantly sees the ape in us and is interested in the parts of our bodies that we scratch with either hand, because this is one of the most conservative patterns of animal behaviour. Most animals have a special way of scratching and certain areas are always scratched in a particular way. In these discoveries of the zoologists, the interesting thing is that such scratching patterns are more conservative and are preserved longer than even the organs of the body. Nature can more easily change the organs of the body than the pattern of behaviour!

In this connection Lorenz mentioned a bird which has lost

its wings in the course of the ages and with them, of course, the ability to fly. Most birds in the process of scratching bring the leg over the wing and this bird, though it has no wings, still makes this complicated swing when scratching, thereby affording proof of the above theory. It is even possible for zoologists to decide upon the species to which an animal or bird belongs by its way of scratching. The human also has definite patterns of behaviour, for instance, certain gestures made instinctively when trying to develop an idea. Much of our behaviour is still derived from the animal realm. One could collect all these patterns which we show in our typical behaviour just as the animals do. The difference for us is that we are in the fortunate situation of being able to watch what goes on inside us while doing these things; we can watch ourselves from inside and outside, which we cannot do in the case of the queen bee or a dog.

Therefore Dr. Jung makes the following division: in the body we have instincts defined as actions, or types of actions. At the same time, while performing such instinctual actions, we have mental images, emotions, etc., which we experience "from within." These emotions, ideas, and mental images are also typical and collective, just as much as the "modes" of action. Sometimes the emphasis of our experiences lies more in the physical realm, in the instinctual action itself, and sometimes more in its accompanying fantasies and emotions. For instance, you can do something in the physical realm and be so wholly absorbed by it that there is practically no psychological conscious reaction. Normally when you eat you have inner sensations, but you can get so hungry that you become quite unconscious until you have swallowed a certain quantity of food; then you wake up and feel better—the ape in you just grabbed and ate. At first you had no reactions and were drowned in the action of eating, you were purely animal. In another situation, when sitting at your writing desk thinking, you are completely centred in this archetypal pole, except

51

for some instinctive scratching perhaps, with a relative inactivity in the other realm.

Normally you move between the two poles. The feeling of life moves between the two and all life activity in this realm we would call "psychic" and would include consciousness plus unconsciousness. These two poles have a secret connection. You may see, for instance, especially when people do something creative, that an idea does not always well up in its realm directly, but through an activity in the body. If you are trying to draw, the image may start completely in the physical realm and only later be represented on paper. Analysands can sometimes only express a thing by a physical gesture and in performing the gesture they realize the psychic content; they do not know in advance what will be expressed but have to move with the feeling. On the other hand, if in one realm there is an inhibition, perhaps impotence in a man, where the physical instinct cannot work, very often by putting straight the ideas he may have about sexuality—i.e., treating the thing simply from the aspect of the ideas—the other sphere can be straightened out also. That would mean that sometimes one realm can activate the other. They are probably one and the same life phenomenon.

There is not absolute freedom of choice in the life of an individual as to where the emphasis is to be put. For example, X falls in love with Y. Practically, there would be choice as to whether the relationship shall be lived out on the platonic or the physical level. Modern man has the illusion that he can choose whether, for instance, he should live the archetypal idea of the union of the opposites in the physical or the spiritual way, or in the in-between realm where both are included. That seems to be in the hands of the individual. But if you have analysed the dreams of people in such a situation, you will see that the unconscious often takes a very definite stand about the level on which this should be lived and makes definite taboos against one sphere or the other. If the individual makes a mistake and decides to live the pattern on a wrong level, the whole relationship may go on the rocks. An individual may, for instance, decide to live it out on the spiritual realm and thereby become very neurotic. The unconscious makes the definite decision—it is not exactly our own choice. One has to watch the dreams and feel one's way along. Sometimes there is an oscillation from one pole to the other.

The mistakes one makes by not having the right balance can be recognized by various feelings, or if there is a bad deviation then neurotic symptoms can come up. Therefore there must be an unknown regulating factor which decides the level or field on which these experiences should be lived. It is likely that this regulating centre coincides with the whole regulating centre of the individual, i.e., the Self. If you accept this idea, then it becomes clear what cursing a human being by transforming it into an animal really means: it is a mistake, an over-balance towards the body-pole, i.e., the infra-red pole. Something which should be lived more in the psychic or spiritual field, is obliged to be lived on the animal pattern. In the case of a warm-blooded animal, if a content of the unconscious is represented as having to behave like an animal, and should not do so, this would mean that there is a psychological concept which should be lived in the middle realm, but that for certain specific reasons it has been forced towards one of the poles; that is the disturbance which has to be straightened out.

Fairytales represent this as a human being over which an animal skin has been thrown, so that there is only an animal expression of behaviour. One has to ask why that should be so. In practical cases, generally such unfortunate deviations happen because in the conscious realm the individual has a conception of life which does not agree with his own setup, which is why psychotherapy can be of use in such cases. By putting straight the conscious attitude the deviation can be stopped and the general values of the individual can be restored.

By a curse the individual may be transformed into a cold- or warm-blooded animal, or into a bird which flies away and cannot be caught. Birds in general, because of their evasiveness, are fantasy or spiritual contents of the psyche, hence the idea that souls of the dead have wings and may appear in bird form. If, therefore, someone is transformed into a bird you may say that something is being expressed only as an idea whereas there should be a total human experience.

One tends to have the views of life and of reality in general which block off one or the other pole. If you are an ascetic, or a Christian monk, then you try to block off the body-pole, which must not be lived. You may go to the fringe of experience but afterwards there is a taboo. If you are a materialistic Communist, you block off the spiritual pole by thinking there is no such thing as the psyche, that man and the meaning of individual life is bunk; you consist of just a body and certain typical reactions. In this case the archetypal pole is blocked off with a prejudice or conscious decision that things are so. If you are not punished with a neurosis, then you have the *Weltanschauung* which agrees with your make-up, but if you are punished by restlessness, etc., then you have to find out whether you are living as you should. These are extremes of attitudes by which you can see the two poles. Most people live between the two. If something is blocked off somewhere and if a spiritual being wants something, you may dream that a ghost would like to enter another body, to be reincarnated in another being, in which case you can assume that there is a content activated on one side of the scale which wants to enter into the sphere of the human.

There is a Chinese ghost story about the spirit of suicide. Some Chinese peasants believe that there is a spirit of suicide and that such a demon after killing one person goes on to another. Among children, or primitive people, if one child or person commits suicide there is the danger of a chain reaction and hundreds can be infected with the same idea. The Chinese,

54

therefore, speak of the demon of suicide who tries to lure people to self-destruction and who goes round with a string in his hand. The story goes that a soldier, while walking about, looks through a window and sees a very sad looking woman sitting beside a cradle in which there is a child. She seems to be in despair, but he does not know why. He looks up and sees at the ceiling the suicide demon dangling a string in front of the woman. He sees how the eyes of the woman look up and realizes what will happen next. He therefore enters and attacks the demon, but the latter is a ghost so that the soldier only hits his own nose instead of the demon and he loses a lot of blood. Somehow the human blood seems to be the charm, for at this moment the demon shouts and disappears. The soldier then discovers that the string with which the demon lured the people to suicide has turned into a string of red flesh round his arm, it has become a part of his own flesh. The soldier is then rewarded as a great hero.

Here it is as if an autonomous psychological impulse of mental or thought quality only stopped its destructive activity when it got in touch with the soul of the human being, by whose blood and the hanging of the cord around the human being's arm it was incarnated. This is, of course, a symbol of the Self. The destructive activity of the symbol of the Self is stopped and replaced by its healing quality.

When people are in a suicidal mood they project onto death the realization of the Self and this projection supports them in committing suicide. They think they will have peace and that they will be out of their conflicts, etc; that is, they project the Self onto death. The suicidal idea is a destructive aspect of the symbol itself, and in the fight with the soldier it became transformed and its further destructive activity bound. Its future activity would be born out of the realization of the Self and that is why the soldier becomes the great hero, for the destructiveness of the cord is stopped. This is the symbol of the round thing. It had been activated in one realm and wanted to enter the sphere of human relationship. If you resist, and block off, and say you don't believe in such things, then the destructive influence poisons the effect of the active archetypal contents just as badly as if you repressed a genuine physical instinct through certain prejudices.

[Here the question was put as to why physical treatment should affect the psyche.]

In catatonic states, treatment with drugs such as mescaline may temporarily improve the condition of the patient. You break the block through shock and the whole thing begins to flow. After an electric shock people become fluid again. The only fact I know about physical treatment is that after having deblocked the thing by this means, if a digestive process takes place in the psyche, then you can talk about a cure having started on the physical side. If not, you have the process of the habitual "electro-shockist." There are people who cannot be without it. To them it is like taking opium. At the Burghölzli mental hospital in Zurich they have statistics on the schizophrenics sent home after shock treatment, and those given psychotherapy after the shock, showing how often each class of patient returns. This has been done now for a period of over ten years and shows quite clearly that those patients who receive psychotherapeutic treatment do not return as frequently as the others. Therefore it is seen that the important thing is the psychological digestion of the effect. If you digest what you experience, it is helpful, otherwise nothing definite happens.

Dr. Jung has been asked whether one could not give Communists mescaline so that they could no longer deny the reality of spiritual experience. His attitude is that if there is an invasion of unconscious contents, which is what happens under mescaline, it has no effect if it cannot be digested. Therefore we do not wish for such a thing to take place because we believe the unconscious knows how much to hand to the person. If patients have no archetypal dreams then stand off from the

56

unconscious for this shows that there is no capacity for digesting it.

I would say that any kind of physical treatment is welcome unless it damages. Patients who have had shock treatment tend to give up the hope that they might cope with their own illness themselves; it discourages them from thinking that they can do something themselves and after shock treatment you have to fight this attitude. You have to say: "No, this time you must fight it yourself." They are much more discouraged than if you had had them in therapy from the beginning.

We have often observed that the fighting instinct and capacity for digestion, or the attitude for wishing to digest, has been weakened through physical treatment. One should use it only with great circumspection and care, and where there is no other possibility, e.g., in catatonic cases. It is better than nothing, but the dangers should be borne in mind and another time the patient must try to stand the thing and not be overdependent on the shock. The ability to hope makes a tremendous difference. It means giving oneself a chance. Shock therapy is felt like an exclusion of the "grace of God."

I think that in a civilization whose main dominants are the Buddhist or Judeo-Christian religions, it is likely that certain instincts would be repressed onto the animal level since there is a tendency to depose certain aspects; for instance, the anima appears as an animal because she is not accepted. There are stories which confirm this. There is an Irish story about mermaids who before the time of the Christian missionaries in Ireland were human beings and the daughters of a pirate chief. When the missionaries came he decided that his daughters should not be their brides so they disappeared into the sea as mermaids and have lured men to disaster ever since. Here there is clearly a regression of the anima into the animal form. But against this is the fact that in very primitive civilizations, where we know that there is no such prejudice against the body, you find the same thing, namely human beings bewitched and transformed into frogs or snakes. This threw into question my theory for a time, and I had to ask how it worked.

If you study the whole setup of such primitive situations you will see that they are just as likely as we to make the same mistake, i.e., to interpret something as psychological when it is physical and vice versa. There are doctor animals and ordinary animals, and they are uncertain as to which is which. This uncertainty as to what should survive seems to be a general human condition. There exists a very deep-seated possibility of error and uncertainty as to the level on which certain impulses have to be lived and classified. It may happen that a primitive hunter shoots a bear and is afterwards horrified to discover that he has shot an ancestral ghost. He did not experience quickly enough the psychic implications. I think this must have to do with the fact that we do not consciously grasp our threshold instinctive reactions; we always tend to keep within ourselves threshold reactions such as a little doubt, or a little impulse not to do something. If the impulses are not very strong we are inclined to put them aside in a one-sided way and by this we have hurt an animal or a spirit within us. This we do practically constantly, as apparently even primitives do, for in the passion of hunting they forget. They say afterwards that they knew they should not have shot the animal but that they forgot for a minute and this, I imagine, is a very general human phenomenon. Man is preconditioned to skip his instincts and his spiritual impulses through the fact of having consciousness.

Last time I left a point unsolved. I put a question about a human being who had been bewitched and turned into a tiger and said that the human instinct would not be to behave like a tiger. Therefore what would it mean if an impulse appeared in a dream as a wolf or a tiger? Here a psychological content has been wrongfully pushed into the body side and perverted so that it is no longer typically human.

58

It is a fact that if an impulse from one or the other sphere comes up and is not lived out, then it goes back down and tends to develop anti-human qualities. What should have been a human impulse becomes a tiger-like impulse. For instance, a man has a feeling impulse to say something positive to someone and he blocks it off through some inhibition. He might then dream that he had driven over a child with his car—he had had a spontaneous feeling impulse on the level of a child and his conscious purpose had smashed it. The human is still there, but as a hurt child. Should he do that habitually for five years, he would no longer dream of a child who had been hurt but of a zoo full of raging wild animals in a cage. An impulse which is driven back loads up with energy and becomes inhuman. This fact, according to Dr. Jung, demonstrates the independent existence of the unconscious.

No one has seen what the unconscious is; it is a concept, not an ectoplasmic reality somewhere in space. If something comes into my mind from my unconscious, a moment later it can fall below the threshold of consciousness: I know the man is Mr. So-and-So, a minute later I have forgotten the name, and afterwards I may remember it again. Therefore, one can assume that what is unconscious is that which is not associated with ego consciousness. If you observe a content which then disappears for a short time into the unconscious, it is not altered when it comes up again, but *if you forget something for a long time, it does not return in the same form*; it autonomously evolves or regresses in the other sphere, and therefore one can speak of the unconscious as being a sphere, or entity, in itself. It is really something like a liquid in which the contents are transformed; you can even see when a content comes up in bad shape and can tell how long it has been repressed and therefore become suspect. Severe repressions may appear in a dream as an evil-smelling corpse in a cemetery, one which has had to be dug up. Something has been repressed for so long

59

that it has disintegrated and decayed in the earth. Indirectly, therefore, you can say that the unconscious psyche is a reality of its own.

If a tiger, wolf, or bear skin is thrown over a content of the psyche, the type of animal chosen simply expresses the form in which it tends to behave but should not, for it should be human. Some people have a wild affect and may dream of going berserk. As long as they dream about a real bear you have to be patient, but if the same person dreams about the human being behaving like a bear then you have to say, "No, you should be able to behave in a human way." It may have been impossible formerly, but now they should be able to control their rage, it is wrong for a human being to behave like a bear! At first the content appears as a real animal and if the dream shows an animal which can speak or do things like a human, then the content can be assimilated on the human level. But if the dream speaks of the man going berserk or wearing a bear skin you could say that now the dreamer should defend himself in a human way instead of going wild.

The very fact that fairytales speak of a person being bewitched shows that their animal condition is no longer legitimate. Some patients, for instance, make hysterical scenes and one knows one has to bear it because they are forced to behave like that, but then suddenly you begin to feel that this is no longer legitimate, now a stage has been reached where such scenes should stop. Very often people have got into a bad habit and because it has been accepted by the analyst for a time they continue in it, but then comes the time for you to say that they should now shed the animal skin, though you may have fully accepted it before. So it is a question of timing, and there we come to one of the key problems of the redemption motif, the problem of time. In order to be less theoretical, I will tell you a short version of a longish Russian fairytale called "The Frog Who Was a Czar's Daughter."

A Russian czar has three sons and when they are grown up

he tells them to take a silver bow and a copper arrow and to shoot as far as they can; wherever the arrows alight, there will be their brides. The eldest son gets a daughter of a czar, the second a daughter of a duke, and in each case the son marries the girl who has brought back the copper arrow. The youngest son shoots and the arrow falls into a swamp and a frog brings back the arrow and insists on being married. The old czar says that all his future daughters-in-law must make cakes and that there must be a competition. The youngest son goes to the frog and cries, but the frog makes the best cakes. Then linen has to be woven, and the frog wins again, and the third test is to show which is the most beautiful. The frog says to her bridegroom: "Go home and have confidence in me and you will see. When it begins to rain you must say that your bride is washing, and when it thunders and lightning flashes, you must say that now she is putting on her clothes." He does this. Again the others all laugh, mocking him. But the door opens and in comes a beautiful woman, more beautiful than any of the others.

At the banquet the former frog puts a part of the food into her sleeve. The others think this funny, but do the same. When the food falls out of the frog princess's sleeve, it is transformed into a beautiful tree with a big black tomcat who sings and tells fairytales. The others do the same thing with the food, but it flies into the czar's face and he is very angry. The youngest son is happy with the redeemed bride who is no longer a frog. He goes up to his room and sees the frog skin lying on the floor. He takes it and throws it into the fire. The bride comes in and says that now he has ruined everything and that she has to go, but that perhaps he will find her again if he is very clever. He goes to a famous witch—the Baba Yaga— who shows him the way. So he comes to the end of the world, beyond the big sea, and there he finds his bride sitting in a glass palace behind iron, silver, and golden doors, in great grief. He saves her and they escape the persecutions of the dragon who owns the palace. She had been cursed by her father and forced to serve this dragon, but now she is redeemed. There, as you see, the great catastrophe comes through the burning of the frog skin.

Another story, Italian, goes as follows. The king of England marries the queen of Hungary and they have a child which is called Prince Pork because he comes into the world as a pig. Three Fates appear at the cradle: the first gives him good moral qualities, the second beauty, but the third says that he must live as a pig. So he lives the life of a pig. When he is twenty, the parents want to find a bride for him and go to a poor washerwoman who has three beautiful daughters. The eldest daughter thinks that she would get a lot of money and that she could kill the pig, so she decides to accept, but he notices her knife and kills her first. The same thing happens with the second daughter. The third daughter, who is gentle and kind, also agrees but she does not plan to kill the pig. She is kind to him, and when her mother-in-law asks how she likes being married to a pig, she says one should love what one has. At night the pig always sheds his skin and turns into a beautiful prince. One day the parents enter the room and see the pig's skin on the floor. They throw it into the fire and from then on he is redeemed. In this story, the burning of the skin is the means of redemption, while in the first the burning of the skin nearly ends in a terrible catastrophe. I have taken these two stories because they illustrate opposite means of redemption, but there are many such stories which contradict each other.

Therefore you have the questions as to the right method and the meaning of the burning of the animal skin. Should it be done or not? We know that for a human being to have to walk about in an animal skin implies a curse and a wrong state of affairs. If we make a comparison with psychological facts, it could mean that a certain complex which could function in a human conscious form is arbitrarily repressed and so compelled to behave in a perverted animal form. Therefore one could say that the animal skin should be burnt, but in one story this is not the case. In the first story the prince has done nothing and has to do his part as an act of love and devotion. In the pig story the girl had done this and the final act is the burning of the skin.

It looks as though it were not possible simply to throw away the skin but as if a long effort towards consciousness would be required to enable the complex to continue to function in a human way. I would say that ultimately it depends on the maturity of the conscious attitude. If the latter is fit to integrate the content, the animal skin can be burnt, and if not, then it cannot. The curse has actually been caused by a prejudice which hitherto has not been worked out. Until the conscious attitude has matured and changed its attitude towards the complex, the burning of the animal skin in itself does not help.

A change in the conscious attitude has always to be worked out first by a human effort and with human devotion. The cause of the curse has otherwise not been removed and may always come back; i.e., the childishness of the conscious personality may bring up the neurotic situation again. It is not only a question of the therapy of the symptoms, but the development of the whole conscious personality, as otherwise another symptom may appear; therefore the prejudice or narrowness of the conscious attitude has to be changed and not only the symptom attacked.

Lecture 5

We have discussed the motif of the animal skin, which in the Italian story, "King Porco," was burnt, thus bringing about the redemption of the pig prince. In the Russian story, on the other hand, when the bridegroom burns the frog skin of the princess the latter is not redeemed, but has to leave him, telling him that he has ruined everything and that now he will have to search for her again in a long quest, taking him literally to the end of the world. When at last he does find her there she says that had he not come then it would have been too late.

In the first version the partner had given the pig prince, King Porco, a lot of loving devotion before the skin was burnt, while in the second the bridegroom had not previously done anything. Therefore, obviously, just to burn the skin seems not to be sufficient, for either before or afterwards some additional effort has to be made.

If we discuss the symbolism of this motif we first have to realize what the burning of the animal skin would really mean. Fire generally refers to emotion. There are ample similes for this interpretation: when one is in love, one is "set on fire"; rage is compared to "a raging fire," and so on. On a minor scale, if fire is not destructive but used for cooking, it may stand for loving attention, which would mean emotional participation in the problem. If the animal skin is burnt and destroyed we might therefore say that this is the moment when one attacks the unconscious complex emotionally. One can either do that within oneself, or it can be done to one, for instance in analysis, or by a partner, whenever there is an emotional attack upon the other person's unconscious.

64

In analysis it is possible to point out to an analysand for a long time that something is wrong and should be cleared up— if the dreams point in that direction—but the realization does not seem to penetrate. You have the feeling that the analysand does not realize it in the totality and needs an electric shock, so to speak. This might come through life, or through the partner, or the analyst. It cannot be planned in advance for that would be ridiculous, even though one knows that sooner or later it is inevitable, as the person has not fully grasped the thing; it remains as an idea, or as a little thing of no great importance, and the way in which the complex actually works is not realized. Sometimes when I think that I must do something about such an unsatisfactory condition, then that very day the analysand comes and has received just such a shock from another person.

It is as though the thing had worked up to bursting point, where life provides the shock if the analysis does not: it is the moment for the animal skin to be burnt away. On occasions it appears to me to be advisable to give, or produce, the emotional shock myself and not wait until it reaches the analysand through life. This situation arises where it might be too dangerous if the thing were left to fate, as something might happen which could destroy more than could be borne at that time; whereas if you apply the shock yourself, by providing your own emotional participation you keep the situation in hand and within a human framework.

By observing one's own reactions one can tell when an emotion is building up, and one must then think carefully whether it would not be better to act rather than wait for the shock to come from another side, with the possible risk that harm may result. I think it is wise at such a time to let out one's own affects as a "gift of friendship," for basically it is a friendly act when you give a fellow human being a negative affect— but only if you yourself are not obsessed by it!!! If the analyst is obsessed by it, then there is no merit in expressing it, but if you could just as well swallow your negative affect, then there is an ethical problem. One *could* be detached, but if so, the partner is robbed of the immediate warmth of a low animal kind of participation. In these cases, to be Christian and understanding and detached is no good; one needs a more subtle kind of warmth, for one is more related, and more humble, when one lets out immediate emotion and gives the other person the affect and emotional participation which one feels.

In this way you can sometimes burn away the animal skin and destroy the unrelated blindess, due to the state of obsession of the other person. If one has enough rapport in the relationship, it is sometimes the only way to help the person to a realization of certain complexes. Either before or afterwards the problem has to be worked out on another level for, after such a shock, at least the next few analytical hours will be given to discussing it, because naturally the other person will reproach you for having let out an affect.

It sometimes happens the other way round and the state of obsession is hollowed out from underneath. The analysand may behave like a blind animal, being obsessed by an unconscious content, and you may think that this is a genuine reaction. But after a time the habit of becoming emotional begins to look rather theatrical. Here you have the complex with the animal skin over it. Sometimes you think the analysand has moved out secretly, though on the surface the old habit remains. Now you could crush it, and often you hear afterwards that he knew the thing should have stopped before but had not the strength to do it himself.

Children too sometimes have childish habits which you can see have been nearly outgrown, but an additional jolt is necessary to help them make the last step. That would mean working first on the complex and then burning the animal skin, while the other way would be first giving the shock and then burning the skin. In each case you can say that there is a separation between the complex and its mode of manifestation,

66

for the animal skin is a way of expression which *was* once genuine, but has simply become an habitual expression and no longer really expresses the complex. You can observe such a thing sometimes with people who have phobias—say a desire to arrange things on a table. At first they are completely driven, but after a certain time in analysis when they still keep up the old habit you are obliged to tell them to stop it. Earlier this would have been impossible, but it does help at the end of an analysis, when it would mean the burning away of the last remnants of the negative complex so that the energy hitherto in the symptom could be switched over to other activities in life.

In the Russian fairytale the princess disappears in a specific way. She appears first as a frog and then slowly becomes human. But when the bridegroom burns the skin she disappears and he has to find her again at the end of the world, in a palace made of glass in a wood beyond the sea. Here he has to go through an iron, a silver, and a golden door, behind which she is sitting weaving and crying. She says, "If you had not come soon you would never have seen me again." This is a strange motif, but a very typical situation which happens frequently in redemption stories.

Last time we discussed the scheme of psychic events, or psychological life, as comparable to the spectrum with its two poles, the one (infra-red) being the body with its instinctual balance, and the other (ultra-violet) the archetypes or ordering spirit.

The assumption is that the two poles are probably two different aspects of the same thing, but can only be described from one or the other angle. One might say that the point of unity would be the transcendental reality of the human being. In our story the anima is first constellated in that reality. She could not enter the psychic realm at once. Why could she not manifest to the prince in a dream? Why has she first to go into a swamp and appear as a frog? Why not in a human form? The story says it is because she had been cursed by her father; we do not know for what reason, but it probably has to do with the *Weltanschauung* of the whole human being. If I have a basic attitude in consciousness which makes it impossible for certain psychic contents to penetrate it, then they must make a detour to get at me. If one is incapable of perceiving that there is such a thing, then the unconscious cannot bring out the content either. In the story, there was a block against the anima. Disturbances, dreams, and symptoms can be produced, but the unconscious has no means of making itself understood if in the conscious there is no attitude adequate to receive the message.

That happens in civilizations where there is a certain narrowness in the collective attitude, making it impossible for the new thing to manifest adequately. For instance, in the dreams of modern North American Indians such as those Paul Radin relates in his books, and in rituals which have only lately been altered, you can see how the unconscious tries to give the Indians a way to adapt to the invasion of white civilization. The latter has been a complete psychological catastrophe for the Indians and they have no means of adaptation, it is something they cannot cope with. In their dream lives there is an attempt in the unconscious to help them, but their conscious *Weltanschauung* is absolutely incapable of listening adequately because their way of interpreting dreams is completely concretistic, and therefore they do not understand the dreams on the right level, i.e., psychologically. They would need a creative medicine man of their own tribe to invent a new method of dream interpretation and help them to understand what is going on in their unconscious. Again, there is a block and therefore though the unconscious makes an attempt to cure the difficulty, it cannot make itself heard because there is no adequate means of interpretation; their *Weltanschauung* makes it impossible to bring up certain necessary experiences.

The negative reaction of the repressed complex does not

appear directly; it is another archetype, the wizard, who curses the anima, for he is angry at not being recognized. Due to the *Weltanschauung,* the archetype of the anima is in a situation where it cannot break into consciousness otherwise, and therefore the attempt is made via the body and the anima appears as a frog in a swamp, which points to that pole of realization.

There is an Algonquin story where the great god wants to give the tribe certain secrets and medicine rituals. To do this he does not call the medicine men together, but he teaches the fish, otter, and other small water animals; he gives them the secret, and it is they who teach the human being. According to that motif the god was not capable of teaching man directly, but had to teach the animals which, in turn, could teach the human. Psychologically, this means that there is probably no nuclear idea or conception in the minds of the Indians by which they could have understood; they have to learn through the instinctual movements of the body, which is what we too try to do in analysis when we ask people to do active imagination and follow mainly physical instinctual impulses. When there is a question of bringing up deeply buried contents of the unconscious one must sometimes make random movements with a pencil and paper. Afterwards the fantasy material becomes richer, but the first start has been made through the body. Actually, the wisdom of such a content, or its message, is buried in the body. It seems to me that this is very typical of the way in which the primitive realizes certain things, namely by playing physically with certain objects until the fantasy ties in.

There is a primitive myth about the invention of the bow and arrow, an ancestral myth. It is said that there was a bow ancestor whose wife was the string who always hung round his neck by her arms, in an eternal embrace. They showed themselves to human beings like that and thus man learned how to make the bow and arrow and to shoot. The two then dis-

69

appeared into the earth. Thus for the invention of the complete instrument there was first a deeply unconscious archetypal fantasy material, and it was that, according to their own report, which brought about the invention. I am convinced that most of the great inventions of man have been triggered by such playful archetypal fantasy material. They are always ascribed to divine powers and divine magic, not only to utilitarian motifs, for it was known that they had their origin in the impulses of the unconscious. Most of the great creations of the present day come initially through dreams and instinctual impulses.

Sometimes if you are confronted with a situation where something is concealed and you do not know what, the only thing to do is to walk about, picking up anything which attracts your attention, trying to find out what energy goes into, meanwhile watching yourself to see what attracts the psychic energy, and then playing with that thing, even if it seems to be quite ridiculous. If you let your fantasy play into the object, then you can bring up what was in the unconscious. This primitive attitude of playing in a childish way is very creative.

If the anima, therefore, sits as a frog in a swamp and attracts the copper arrow of the young czar, I would assume that there is a physical impulse in the unconscious. The human often appears in the bewitched form of a frog, which has definite similarities to the human body; it has little hands and feet and is, on the level of a little cold-blooded animal, like a caricature of the human being. We often call little children little frogs. If an unconscious content appears as a frog, I always conclude that it could become conscious, even that it *wants* to do so. There are contents of the unconscious which are evasive, and which resist being made conscious, but this relative similarity of structure of the frog to the human body affords a fitting symbolic expression for something which is partly buried in the somatic layers of the unconscious, but which has a definite stimulus towards conscious realization.

70

The frog attracts the copper arrow—an amusing motif, since the bow and arrow play a great role in love symbolism.

Laurens van der Post has a little bow and arrow made by the Bushmen of the Kalahari Desert. There, if a young man is interested in a girl he makes such a little bow and arrow. The Bushmen can store fat in their behinds, which stick out, and they can live on this fat in hard times. The young man shoots the arrow into that part of the girl's body. She takes it out and looks to see who has shot it; if she accepts the young man's attentions she goes to him and hands him back the arrow, but if not, she takes the arrow and breaks it and stamps on it. They still use Cupid's arrow! You see why Cupid, the god of love in antiquity, had a bow and arrow!

We can interpret the arrow psychologically as a projection, or projectile. If I project my animus onto a man it is as though a part of my psychic energy would flow towards that man and at the same time I would feel attracted to him. This acts like an arrow, an amount of psychic energy which is very pointed. It suddenly establishes a connection. The arrow of the Bushmen of the Kalahari Desert says to the girl, "My anima libido has fallen on you," and she accepts it or not. But she does not keep the arrow, she brings it back; i.e., he has to take back the projection, but through it a human relationship has been established. The whole symbolism of marriage is contained here.

Copper is the metal of the planet Venus (Cypris of the island of Cyprus), the Venus metal. It has to do with the problems of love and the goddess Venus. The frog picks the arrow up and the relationship is established. Verdigris, the poison of the copper metal, has been interpreted by the alchemists as the dangerous aspect of the principle of love. Copper can easily become poisonous, for it is very quickly affected by outer influences; it is a dangerous metal, it is soft and malleable but it has a poisonous quality. It can also be used for making alloys and that too fits in with the love quality; it can easily be bound or connected with other metals, just as love binds

71

people together. Probably it was because of its capacity for *union* that this metal was attributed to the goddess Venus. The soft metals are usually feminine and the hard metals masculine.

The anima, the frog princess, demonstrates to the court at the dinner party that she is not really a frog. She has supernatural powers, makes wonderful cakes, can weave linen, appears as the most beautiful woman, and from the food stored in her sleeve there grows the tree with the cat on it which can sing songs and tell fairytales. She thus shows that, though she had to appear first in that inadequate way, she is not a frog, but a supernatural divine being, a goddess who can transform the elements. She can also produce a tree, like a wizard, which can appear and disappear, a gift she probably inherited from her father. We could say that she is the one who transforms all reality into a meaningful pattern where art, beauty, and feeling are like the creative manifestations of the archetypal images. The anima provides man's life with both illusion and disillusion. She gives it its feeling of meaningfulness and is inspiration for his creative fantasies. How man reacts to the anima depends on his attitude.

In our story it is unfortunate that the whole production of the anima figure only appears at the dinner party. There is a tendency not to value this manifestation rightly. If such a thing happened in reality one should really fall on one's knees and ask what is behind it. The relatively light reaction produced towards this manifestation of the goddess is probably responsible for the fact that the prince so thoughtlessly burns the skin, that she disappears to the end of the world, and that so much effort has to be made to find her again. This is always the case, and very typical, when the man accepts the influences and manifestations of the anima only aesthetically and does not take her seriously ethically.

In outer life that would be to relate to the woman as a kind of Don Juan, just flirting with her—a dinner party in a fairytale. Many artists write or paint beautifully, but if you ask them the meaning of what they have done they run away, saying that psychological interpretation destroys the work of art. This is an attitude common to many modern artists who do not want to be hit by the seriousness of what they have produced. Therefore they try to leave it in the realm of artistic amusement and really "play at a dinner party." So we can say that the original difficulty, namely a certain prejudice in consciousness, still exists, which accounts for the whole thing breaking up as soon as the skin is burnt. The conscious attitude is not taking the anima seriously, and therefore the catastrophe occurs and the young czar has to make the long quest to find her again.

The interesting thing is that when he finds her she is sitting in a palace in the woods, obviously in a structure which we would interpret as a symbol of the Self in its more feminine aspect. It would typify the mystical experience within the soul, as described in the writings of the Christian mystic, Thérésa of Avila, in which an "interior castle" of gold and silver is the famous image for the innermost centre of the psyche which we call the Self.

In this castle there is also a dangerous being which does not appear. It is not clear whether it is the father wizard, or a dragon. The girl is in his power and the bridegroom has to fetch her and run away with her quickly, as something dangerous would happen otherwise. If you compare this with other stories, you will see that this dangerous figure is generally with the devil. This is a strange compensatory process for the fact that there is an undervaluation of the anima figure in the unconscious. She gets contaminated with the image of God in its dark side.

The more a man does not realize the value of the anima in consciousness the more she tends to become either diabolical, or identical with the whole unconscious and the image of God. It is as though he had to put her unconsciously on a throne

73

and worship her, just because he is not conscious enough. It is like a diabolical possession, which is subjectively experienced as religious emotion.

You can observe this if you study a Nazi. Nazis, or Communists, do not recognize inner psychic facts as such, because consciously they are only interested in sociological theories. Their emotional life therefore falls into the unconscious and ties itself up with an unconscious image of God; that results in the strange "religious" fanaticism you find in all such movements. They are even willing to die for it, or to burn up the whole world. Why, if it is only a national political programme? You will always find that what they really project into their political ideas is the Kingdom of God. They want to establish it on earth "in the right way," and therefore they have the right to destroy everybody else, to murder a few thousands. If you talk to such people you find this to be their unconscious emotional attitude. They are mostly possessed, and project the image of God with which their whole idealistic emotion is tied up—that is an example of the contamination of the anima with the image of God, where the symbol of the Self tends to become a destructive possession.

A symbol of the Self, or image of God which is not recognized, is most destructive because it then becomes a force acting from behind which causes destructive emotions and mass prejudices of all kinds. That is why it is difficult to talk to such possessed people in a reasonable way; they are completely emotionally tied up with the image of the Self, which they do not realize because they are incapable of looking at themselves psychologically—it is all outside in projection. This regression of the anima figure is a dangerous, destructive fact. The princess says: "If you had not come now you would never have seen me again"—i.e., the whole real psychological development would have died, and that means the death of the individual as well. Therefore he has to make a long, patient effort to bring up these contents of the unconscious again, for other-

74

wise they manifest only aesthetically and afterwards disappear into the unconscious.

The palace in the woods brings us to alchemical symbolism. Metals are always associated with the planets: iron generally stands for Mars and war; silver is connected with the moon, the feminine, the white principle, the soft metal which can unite easily; while gold is associated with the sun. The glass palace with iron, silver, and gold doors has the four substances of the Self as, for instance, in the making of the philosopher's stone. Iron or lead is the *nigredo*, it leads to silver, which is the *albedo*, the whiteness, where the feminine principle dominates, and afterwards comes gold, i.e., the *rubedo*, the red stage where the gold appears. Glass is a substance which represents the spirit or spiritual matter in a concrete form. But in this story the alchemical symbolism of the Self appears with a negative nuance, and I would prefer here to give all these elements such a negative nuance and say that the anima figure is imprisoned in an inhuman hardness. People nowadays have a negative image of the Self and it is hardening incredibly. Certain Nazis made a sport of trying to kill all their feeling; the artificial, destructive hardening of feeling was supposed to be heroic.

In Jung's paper on "The Psychology of the Transference," he says that as a reaction against becoming dissolved in the masses, the unconscious today tries to bring about in people solidification of the individual. In modern man you can see this tendency to solidify the individual. If that goes wrong, or works unconsciously, then it makes a hardening of which, if they are possessed, they are proud, for their leaders are adamantine; here the solidification of the individual has gone wrong. We can say that we have nowadays only one choice— either to become hardened, destructive individuals and defend ourselves unconsciously that way, or to become more inwardly solid individuals. In the former case we are possessed by the symbolism of the Self instead of being its servants.

75

Thus the four substances refer to the quaternity of the Self, but with a negative nuance: the symbolism becomes destructive if one does not relate properly.

The murderous aspect of the possessed or cursed being is something which we can take up in the next story, a Danish one entitled "King Lindworm." This Celtic-Germanic word means snake or dragon; it is also a water course which has such a shape, like the River Limmat, or the Lindt here in Zürich. It can also mean a big worm, or dragon worm, a king dragon with a snake-like form.

A king and queen have no children. After their wedding night they had found an inscription over their bed in the morning telling them that they would never have any. One day the queen, who is desperate, meets an old woman who says that she will help her. She tells the queen to go to the north-west corner of the garden and take with her a bowl which she must turn upside-down and leave there. In the morning when she takes the bowl away she will find a red and white rose. If the queen eats the red rose, she will have a boy, and if she eats the white one she will have a girl, but on no account must she eat both at the same time as that would lead to a catastrophe.

The queen does as she is told and next morning finds the roses. She thinks, if she eats the red rose and has a boy, that when he grows up he will go to the war and be killed, but if she eats the white, when the girl grows up she will marry. She sees no reason why she should not eat both and have twins. She does so but gives birth not to twins but to a horrible dragon, a male creature. It immediately starts making itself disagreeable and threatens to destroy the castle and eat everybody up if it does not get what it wants. When the king, who has been at the war, returns home, it meets him and greets him as father. The king exclaims: "What, am I your father?" "Yes," answers the dragon, "and if you won't be my father I will destroy you and the castle."

So everybody is dominated by the threats of this dragon.

When it is 20 years old it wants to marry. The king protests that nobody will marry it but the dragon says that if the king does not find a bride for it, it will destroy king and castle. So a beautiful princess is found, but on the wedding night the monster eats her. The same thing happens to the next bride and it becomes difficult to provide him with wives. But the dragon becomes more and more threatening and the king is desperate so he goes to an old shepherd and asks him to give him his daughter. The shepherd does not want to, but has to give in and tells his daughter.

The girl, knowing what to expect, goes off into the woods crying. There she meets an old woman who asks her why she is so sad. The girl tells her that she has to marry the dragon and will be killed, whereupon the old woman offers to help and tells her what to do. When the wedding feast is over and it is time for her to go to the bridal chamber she must put on ten shirts, one over the other, and when the dragon says in the dark that she should take off her shirt, she is to answer that she will but that he should take off a skin. This she must do each time until she has pulled off nine shirts, by which time he will have no more skins to pull off and she will still have one shirt on. He will then lie there like a lump of bleeding flesh and she must beat him with hazel sticks, dipped in the lye she has had put in the room, until he nearly falls into bits, after which she must bathe him in sweet milk and wrap him up in the nine shirts and then she will fall asleep for a short time with him in her arms.

The girl does as she is told and when she wakes up finds that she is in the arms of a beautiful prince who has been redeemed from the curse. Later a villain appears in the story who slanders the princess, but we will concentrate on the first part of the story.

The trouble is brought about by the queen's greed: she wants the penny and the cake. She had thought she would get twins; she might have thought that she would get a hermaphro-

77

dite, a close connection of the dragon. The alchemists speak either of the dragon or the hermaphroditic monster, something monstrous and unnatural and not positive. It has to be cut in pieces, destroyed, or redeemed because it represents a union of the opposites on a too-unconscious level. It refers again to the same motif which we discussed before, the castle into which the frog princess disappears. That is where the human is possessed by the Self instead of being realized and related to the archetype of the Self. You find this often in borderline cases and among people who have got into touch with material of the unconscious through specific study, say of mythology, or primitive people, and so on. These people cannot relate to their material but get possessed by it. They speak "out of the archetype" and "announce" archetypal material like an old medicine man, but they do not link it up with their modern level of consciousness, and they never ask themselves about it.

The archetypal patterns are so meaningful and exert such an emotional grip that such people talk like a book and are drowned in the material instead of understanding it. I refer to the type of person you find in modern civilization, a kind of conceited magician. There are men and women who instead of realizing the contents of their unconscious get possessed by them; then they identify with the archetype of the Self and adopt the pose of the Wise Old Man or the Great Mother. They can always announce the great truth, but if you study what they say and the way they behave, you will see that they are talking out of their possession by the archetype. The material seems to be meaningful, but they have lost the shape of their own personality, they have over-expanded.

Usually there is a connection with the moral attitude of such a person. They are "radio announcers" of the archetype and the feeling function has been destroyed. The condition is almost tantamount to moral insanity. Hitler was such a type. He made a tremendous impact on people, but if you analysed

78

his speeches you saw that he always produced very great truths, which he intuited from the unconscious, mixed up with the most awful immoral junk. But because such pearls of truth came to him through the nearness of the unconscious, people got caught by what he said and did not realize the junk with which it was mixed up.

Though Hitler was a prime example of the type, we meet such people in everyday life, people who have the unethical, shifting attitude which fits the archetype but not the human being; they are frequently not insane, but are "radio announcers" of their unconscious contents, which want to be expressed and which impress those around them. They have a destructive effect. Some people can observe their ethical inferiority, but others, less critical, or those who are not ethically secure, fall into the trap. Such borderline people are those of whom Jung says that the complex of the ego and the archetype of the Self have been contaminated, so that both become blurred. Therefore, the ego displays qualities of the Self which it ought not to have, and the Self takes over qualities of the ego, which should not be in it.

The archetype of the Self we define as the totality of the personality and as such it stands at the beginning of human life. In earliest childhood there is already an unconscious totality, just as the acorn contains the whole tree. Usually in life the ego complex shuts itself away from the Self and only in the second half of life is there an attempt by the ego to cope with the totality of the personality until—to take the ideal case—there is a complete realization of ego and Self as described in Zen Buddhism and other mystical experiences where the ego experiences the Self and becomes one again with it. Sometimes the ego does not separate properly from the Self; the process is disturbed, and consequently the ego does not polarize away from the rest of the unconscious personality, but gets vaguely mixed up with it, and then you have a strange personality, either childish or very wise, more or less conscious

79

than other people, and hopelessly unconscious too—neither fish nor fowl.

To analyse such people is hell, because in one way, having talked of the unconscious, they know all about it; indeed, they are right in it, but if you try to take them off and away from it, they say that they know enough of its value to prevent that happening. There has to be a rebuilding of the feeling value by means of the unconscious. It means long and tedious work; you cannot distinguish the two factors, ego and Self.

If we take the queen who ate first the red rose: she should have given birth to a masculine being, but he is wrongly contaminated with his feminine part, he is a hermaphrodite, wrapped up in what should not belong to him, that is, wrapped up in the feminine or the dragon skin—the anima which surrounds him—in the wrong way. As you know, one of the highest symbols of the Self is Christ surrounded by the Church—*vir a femina circumdatus.* Christ's bride is the Church and at the end, when wholeness is realized, Christ will be completely incarnated in the multitude of the believing Christians, the Church, and therefore "the man surrounded by the woman." The woman is like a circle around the man, the divine being in the middle of the mandala, the Anthropos, standing on a quadrangular form as the idea of the masculine aspect of the Self embedded in the feminine, like Buddha sitting in the lotus flower.

This highest symbol of the human goal has an awful, horrible shadow, a negative aspect, and that would be our dragon prince. It is the same thing when it is wrong and destructive and has not been realized in a conscious way in life, but has caught the human being from behind, with all its destructive instead of constructive aspects. This Prince Lindworm is also the man surrounded by the woman, but he is in the form of a lump of bleeding flesh surrounded by a dragon skin, a regressive form of the union of the opposites.

Such symbols of the Self always appear when there is a

tendency in the individual to solve a problem by regressing to a former stage of civilization. In early Christianity, in the first thousand years A.D., the problem of life and relationship between man and woman first becomes Christianized. Being a patriarchal content it cut off the sexual aspect. Man had the possibility of relating to a real woman through the social institution of marriage—anything else was sin—and of sublimating the rest of his anima figure and projecting it onto the Virgin Mary. If he projected it onto another woman he was in trouble.

This solution of the whole life problem and the problem between the sexes was acute in the 11th, 12th, and 13th centuries. The Christian knights of the time made an attempt to develop the problem of the anima and human relationship through the Courts of Love ("Les Cours d'Amours"), where a man could express his feeling for a woman. These provided an attempt for the man to become conscious of the anima problem. Naturally they got into trouble and there were endless ethical and human complications. At that time the Christian knights kept in touch with the Islamic world, and its institution of a harem seemed to offer a solution, for here there was supposed to be no sexual problem and there were no old maids. Every woman had a man and was sexually satisfied.

The institution of the harem is a good solution, psychologically, since it prevents repression of sexuality, but on the other hand there is nowhere less relationship between man and woman: the men talk to the men and the women to the women. The man addresses the woman only by erotic jokes, a real relationship is unknown in that type of civilization. Still, when the Christian knights got into touch with the harem psychology it was a tremendous temptation to see that as the solution. But that would have been a regression, and therefore you find in myths that they are all threatened by the Islamic world, which appears as a hermaphroditic being.

So, from the material, you can say that it would be a way

out of the difficulty, but that it would be a regression into a former, more primitive state of affairs. This is the great temptation everywhere; instead of groping through into a new solution, there is regression into the former primitive state where there was not yet a problem. That is why some people go to Hawaii, or some other island, thinking to find oneness with nature—a solution in a regressive form, and people become even more neurotic through it, because it is the wrong way.

Lecture 6

We still have to discuss the strange motif in the Danish story of King Lindworm, where the girl who wants to redeem the dragon prince has to wear ten shirts, and every time the dragon bridegroom tells her to take off her shirt she says that he should take off one of his skins until, when he has taken off nine skins and she still has one shirt on, he is left as a whimpering, unhappy bleeding mass of flesh on the floor. Afterwards she whips him with hazel sticks and bathes him in sweet milk, and so redeems him and he becomes a beautiful prince.

I started the interpretation by first trying to show what these many coverings, the many skins covering the true, though unestablished nature of the prince, might mean. I ventured the hypothesis that they represent a complex where the conscious ego and the archetype of the Self are contaminated. I described people in whom the ego is identified with the Self, so that neither the ego of the person nor the archetype of the Self can function properly for, due to the contamination, there has been no adequate polarization of the psyche. This is one aspect of such a figure as the prince covered with many dragon skins, but we can also look at it from another angle. The prince and princess in fairytales often represent those personages who later will become the king and queen, for they are the future king and queen *in statu nascendi,* so to speak.

In *Mysterium Conjunctionis* Dr. Jung devotes a whole chapter to the symbolism of the king in alchemy. As in Egyptian theology and mythology, the king in alchemy represents a dominant of collective consciousness. Whereas the old king represents an over-aged or outworn collective conscious system,

83

the young king usually represents a new symbol of the Self. How is it that the coming king represents the Self while the old king in mythology usually represents a dominant of collective consciousness?

To realize what is meant one must bear historical facts in mind. Buddha, when enlightened under the Bodhi tree, experienced something of the Self, and when confronted with his pupils he became a symbol of the Self for those who surrounded him. Many religious systems crystallized around the figure of Buddha who stood for a divine being, the one divine man, a symbol of the Self. If you study Buddhism in its later stages you can see that Buddha has become a central representation of a religious collective organization, a symbolic idea of what we nowadays call Buddhism and a whole religious system.

You could also say that the figure of Christ has gone through a similar development, for as soon as a symbol of the Self has crystallized, there is only a central representation of the collective system left, and of the symbol which originally represented the real inner experience, only lip service remains. There is left an intellectual or devotional system while the original symbol slowly fades and is petrified into a ritualistic habit. That is what the old king stands for and for this reason he is often represented as the one who resists the new thing which is coming up. When the birth of a divine child is prophesied, the old king trembles, fearing to lose his position. He therefore tries to destroy the child, for though he has himself been a symbol of the Self he has become negative and destructive because, as Jung has shown with a great amount of material in *Aion,* the Self, like all other archetypes, is not only a static nucleus of the psyche, but also a self-renewing system.

If you observe the symbolism of the Self as it manifests in an individual, you will see that it is in a state of constant change. It sheds certain aspects and perpetually renews itself. Jung compares it therefore to certain hydrogen atoms which in higher layers shoot off electrons from time to time and assimilate other electrons. The Self in a human being seems to develop a similar activity; it is a dynamic centre of the psyche which seems to be in a state of constant inner flux. That is why no conscious formulation of an experience of the Self can claim to be absolute over a long period of time—it has to be re-adapted again and again, so as to keep pace with this changing process.

For this reason, religious symbols in general have to be perpetually re-interpreted, and in a living religion there are always dangers of petrification and reforms which rise up in an endeavour to rebuild the original conception and translate it into something more modern and adapted to the needs of a new historical period. You have the same thing in an individual, for even if you have a very deep experience, this may wear out; the truth of yesterday is no longer the truth of today, and what was once a supporting ideal becomes a worn-out system which prevents further inner development. In such a case the truth of yesterday must be set aside for what is *now* the truth of one's own psychic life.

A prince in a fairytale, therefore, usually represents such a symbol of the Self *in statu nascendi* which has to be dug up, or which rises spontaneously from the depths of the collective unconscious. If it is covered with all these skins—as in our story—this means that there is no possibility for this content to appear in its true form, it has first to come up in an animal shape.

You find an analogous situation sometimes in individuals where there is a tremendous instinctive urge or drive. Such a drive possesses people, but one has the uncanny feeling that this is not "it." A man may be in love with a woman and want nothing else, but one feels that it is not really the thing, that he is only possessed by the idea because he cannot realize it, and that if he really did, the whole experience would fall flat. Here the therapist must judge by his own instinct. People do become possessed by something they want and will insist that

85

it is the genuine thing, but one is suspicious for it seems to be only an apparent manifestation of something which lies behind, the central representation is not yet expressed.

In general, it can be said that if a person shows symptoms of being driven or possessed or not free, or unable to sacrifice such a wish, then it is not, or not yet, the real thing. One ought then to assume an expectant, waiting attitude, for where there is such a childish wish you may be sure that something is wrong. One has to wait for the time when the nucleus in the psyche sheds its various manifestations and reveals itself in its true nature.

It is interesting that the girl who wants to redeem the dragon prince has to wear so many shirts. She has to veil herself, and not show herself naked, that is, in her true form. This is a ticklish problem to discuss, but sometimes in analysis one has to feel one's reaction to the analysand when he presents some unreal demand. It cannot just be rejected, for there is something real behind, but one cannot be naive either, for if one exposed oneself in a negative way one would be destroyed or receive a feeling shock or destructive reaction which would harm the relationship. To expose oneself to another's possession has no merit but is rather stupid. One has to be differentiated enough to feel what is genuine, and only relate to that, and keep away from what is not. That is one of the most subtle problems in such a situation.

What the girl says, in effect, is that if the dragon will come out with a more true reaction, then she will answer in the same way, but if he makes a wild, unreal onslaught on her she will be absent. Similarly, if you expose yourself to a possessed demand of an analysand in a naive way, it will only lead to disappointment, for he will feel that he has fallen into a trap. As it is not a genuine thing his better nature will hope that you will not fall for it, and if you do he will turn away; part of him will be dissatisfied, for he has been accepted on a too-naive level.

86

That is how the working out of a complex appears in an analytical relationship, but such a complex can also appear in a single individual and would mean that the conscious attitude should not be hasty in jumping to conclusions, for the unconscious content has many skins and does not appear in its true form. It manifests in dreams in a veiled form, but you may perhaps be able to conclude what lies behind. If the ego has not a subtle enough theory of the unconscious it will take the top veil for the whole truth and then fail to get to the centre of the complex.

Suppose the ego holds Freudian theories and the nucleus expresses itself in a very sexual dream. If your idea is that now we have *it* and this proves not to be the case, then the relationship with the unconscious breaks up and difficulties arise. On the other hand, you need to be sure that the Freudian interpretation is not the right one. Therefore the best reaction is to wear many shirts, i.e., many different attitudes, and to say "for the time being it looks as though." That is, you give the apparent manifestation an adequate theoretical interpretation, but leave the door open for the possibility that there may be a more adequate one. You never know how long the "peeling" may go on or if the level of interpretation is the ultimate one. You have to develop yourself in the process as much as the analysand does, for in a true analysis it is always a simultaneous transformation. You must be ready to shed your mode of interpretation and to give up any theories and hypotheses which you may have about the analysand. You must be prepared to say that the problem is still more complex and wait until there is a realization of the underlying truth. You may ask at such a moment how one can know that the ultimate stage has been reached, but one has an instinct about it; peace of mind can come to both parties, or, if it is only in one's own inner complex, one feels that this is truly *it*. There is generally a lasting feeling and one no longer has the uneasiness which was always around before.

Sometimes when people say that they have a problem and know just what it and its interpretation is, you feel that they are hoping you will agree and at the same time that they do not want you to do so. If there is a lingering malaise within yourself, you may be quite sure that you have not taken off enough shirts and dragon skins and have not reached the naked truth.

In "King Lindworm," the naked truth is this bleeding mass of flesh which has to be exorcised and turned into a beautiful prince. This fairytale represents the compensatory figure of the Self, for the king dragon is that aspect which did not receive sufficient attention in the Christian symbolism. Physical man and the needs of the body did not have a place in early Christianity and have never been adequately dealt with, which is why so many people have left the Church. The development of the symbolism of the Self adds something to our central religious representation, so that it can once more function and certain parts of life can again be drawn into a total attitude. If the Self is the totality of man, then it expresses that part of the human being too, and one must find the answers which help us to live that part of our nature.

A fairytale is true for about three or four hundred years and then generally changes and evolves. If you compare the fairytales of Christian Europe with Chinese or antique fairytales, you will see this. Human consciousness seems to evolve very slowly, and changes in fairytales evolve in the same rhythm. Therefore conscious formulas have to be re-adapted to the living process of the unconscious and the psyche. At least from the psychological standpoint, there is no principle which lasts very long, because of the ever-changing process in the psyche.

That an animal or fleshly disguise covers the true form is a theme also to be found in other civilizations in a very typically different way. A Chinese fairytale called "No Chia" tells of a nobleman and his wife who have no children. The wife,

88

already old— as was Sarah in the Bible—was one day lying in bed when a Taoist priest entered the room with a beautiful pearl. He told her to swallow it and that she would have a child. He then disappeared, and after nine months the woman gave birth to a ball of flesh from which emanated a glowing red light and a wonderful perfume. The husband came into the room and with his sword cut the ball of flesh which turned into a child, a boy.

This boy is very wild, destructive and wicked; he disturbs the dragons under the sea and gets into all kinds of mischief and brings sorrow to his parents and the gods, but in the end he realizes that he must sacrifice himself as compensation. He becomes a god and is worshipped, for he has expiated the evil deeds performed in his youth. Here again is the motif of the symbol of the Self, but manifested much more in the realm of nature. After a long process of self-sacrifice and suffering No Chia becomes a new divine being which replaces the old gods by a new religious symbol.

In alchemical texts it is often said that the divine being is buried and has to be extracted from destructive matter; the *extractio animae* is mentioned in which the minerals have to be heated so that the metal flows out. Into that picture the alchemists projected similar psychological processes, namely that one is concerned with material from the unconscious to which much concentrated attention has to be given (i.e., heat) in order to extract the essentials. That is what we do when we interpret a dream. When people tell their first dreams in analysis they either laugh, or apologize for bringing something which seems to them to be such junk, and they are deeply impressed if you succeed in making an *extractio animae*— getting the essential meaning out of what appeared to them to be merely chaotic material. If the interpretation "clicks," one experiences the life-giving meaning contained in what was seemingly meaningless.

The sword which the king uses represents an act of discrimi-

nation, an intellectual discrimination made when reaching a
decision. I can give you such an example, showing how the unconscious can decide for us. Once when I was uncertain
whether to take on a new analysand, I had a dream in which
a man appeared who had just left his job because he had been
overworked, he could not go on any more. The dream obviously says: "Do not forget that factor within you," and thus it
clarifies the situation. An intellectual discrimination with a
decisive element in it has been reached; the problem has been
dealt with in the instinctive layers of the personality and the
dream announces the decision of the unconscious. Thus decision and discrimination are very closely linked in the *statu
nascendi*. In the Apocalypse, the sword which comes from the
mouth of God is a discriminating factor, and in Alexander's
cutting of the Gordian knot you have the aspect of decision.

A dream, if rightly interpreted, always carries not only an
intellectual enlightenment but a quality of decision, and gives
a different emphasis from that of the conscious. It has ultimately an intellectual *and* ethical effect on the conscious personality. Both the unconscious and the conscious must use the
element of discrimination; the fusion of the two attitudes is
always needed.

Why did the girl put on all those shirts? Why not some
other item of clothing? Clothes have two aspects or meanings.
In one way, they belong to the persona, the mask we show the
world. We dress as we want to show ourselves to our sociological surroundings. In olden days there was a definite dress
for every specific occupation and the whole basic attitude towards life was manifested in the persona. Thus clothes often
veil the true personality and hide the "naked truth."

Hans Andersen tells the story of the king who wanted to
wear the most beautiful clothes. He found a tailor who said
he could make them but that the wrong kind of person would
not be able to see them. Unfortunately the king himself did
not see them, but he was too vain to realize that the tailor was

a fraud and he went out in the street naked. The people knew about the clothes and agreed that he was wonderfully dressed— only a small child said, "But he has no clothes on!" and then everyone began to laugh. Clothes may give a false impression, but it would be too cheap always to interpret them as the mask or persona.

In many mystery cults the true change of the personality is expressed by changing the clothes. Apuleius, when initiated into the Isis mysteries, wore royal garments covered with the signs of the Zodiac, and in early Christian days people put on white garments after baptism to illustrate their renewal and clean attitude. Therefore I would say that clothes usually represent an attitude which one wants to manifest to one's surroundings. People may show a good attitude outside but underneath be full of dirty fantasies and unclean reactions, or, on the other hand, the inner attitude may be cleaner and more true. One talks also of "washing one's dirty linen in public."

The shirt is worn close to the body and usually represents the more intimate attitude. If I dislike Mr. So-and-So I can say that I am pleased to see him, but inwardly I may feel quite differently, and that is the difference between the inner and outer clothing. The shirt represents the attitude which is not yet quite the naked truth, though an intimate one, for it comes between the clothes and the bare skin. It is in this in-between realm in our story of King Lindworm, that the girl has to show herself, nearly in her true nature but not completely so, until the dragon comes out with his real personality at which point she can redeem him. Until then she had to show a genuine reaction but not the ultimate truth.

The shirt also represents a way or means of expression, but I would like to explain this better by telling three other Grimm fairytales which bring up the problem of the shirt in another light.

The first is "The Twelve Brothers." It is about a king and

queen who have twelve boys. The king says if the next child is
a girl he wants to give her all the money and that they will kill
the boys. He has twelve coffins made, with pillows in them for
the heads, and all are put into one room and the door locked
so that the boys should not see them. But the mother is very
unhappy and when her youngest child, Benjamin, asks her why
she is so sad, she tells him and shows him the coffins. He says
that she must not cry, that they will help themselves. They
decide to go to the woods and sit on a tree there and watch.
If a black flag is hoisted, then they will know that a girl has
been born, while a white flag will mean a boy. If the flag is
black they will try to escape. It is the black flag which appears
and the brothers are very angry and vow that if they ever get
hold of the girl they will kill her. They then go into the woods
until they come to a bewitched house where they decide to
stay. Benjamin has to keep house and the others must provide
the food. There they stayed ten years.

Meanwhile the daughter grew up and was kind and good-
hearted. On her forehead was a star. One day she saw among
the washing twelve men's shirts and asked her mother about
them, saying that they were much too small for her father.
The mother tells her and the girl says she must go and find
her brothers and bring them back. So she takes the twelve
shirts and goes into the woods and finds the enchanted house
with Benjamin in it. He is surprised at her beauty and lovely
clothes and the star on her forehead, and asks her where she
comes from and what she is doing there. She tells him that she
is looking for her twelve brothers and shows the shirts. Benjamin is very pleased and kisses her and says they will be recon-
ciled, but says that the brothers have sworn an oath to kill her.
She answers that she is quite ready to be killed for their sake.
Benjamin hides his sister and when the brothers come home
he tells them about her and brings her out. They all make
friends and live together in the house and the sister helps
Benjamin in the work.

One day, wanting to give her brothers a special treat, the girl picks twelve lilies which are growing in the garden and puts one on each plate. But the brothers are immediately changed into twelve black ravens who fly away. The house and garden disappear at the same time, and the girl is left there alone. She does not know what has happened. An old woman appears who tells her that she should have left the lilies in the garden, for they were her brothers who have now been changed for all time into black ravens. The girl asks if there is no way of redeeming them and is told that there is, but a very difficult way, namely that the girl must remain dumb and not speak a single word for seven years. She elects to sit at the top of a tree, but when a young prince goes hunting his dog sees her and barks; the prince falls in love with her and they marry. After a few years the old queen says that this girl is a witch and must be burnt. The girl is tied to a stake and a fire built, but at the moment when it starts to burn the twelve ravens fly back, and as they alight they are turned into human beings. The seven years are exactly up and the girl can explain what happened.

In the story of "The Seven Ravens," a man had seven sons and no daughters and was very pleased when at last a girl was born. But the child was delicate and had to be baptised at once. He therefore sent the boys to fetch water for the baptism, but they broke the jug in which they were to bring it and were too frightened to come home. The father, in his anger, said that he wished they would turn into ravens.

The girl grows up and hears what happened to her brothers, who through her had come to be cursed. Thereafter she has no peace by day or night through thinking of them and finally runs away to look for them. She walks to the end of the world, then to the sun, and afterwards to the moon and the stars. The Morning Star tells her that her brothers are living on a glass mountain, and gives her a little crooked leg with which to open the door of the house where her brothers live. She loses it, but takes a knife and cuts off one of her own

fingers and opens the door with that. A dwarf greets her and
tells her that the ravens are not at home but that she can wait,
and he brings in food and drink for the seven. The girl eats
and drinks a little from each portion and lets the ring she has
brought with her from her parents' home fall into the last
goblet. When the ravens come home they all ask each other
who has eaten and drunk from their food and drink and say
it must have been a human. Then they find the ring and recognize it and say if only their sister were there they would
be redeemed. The sister steps out from behind the door, the
brothers regain their human form, and they all return home
together.

In the next story, "The Six Swans," a king goes hunting in
a big wood where he sees an old woman who will only tell him
the way out of the wood if he promises to marry her daughter.
The girl is beautiful, but he does not like her and soon discovers that he has married an evil witch. The king had had six
boys and a girl by his former wife. Realizing that the new wife
would kill the children, he hides them in a lonely castle in the
middle of a wood and visits them secretly. The witch finds out
and after making six shirts follows the track of the king to
the castle. The boys, thinking it is their father, run to meet
him, whereupon the queen throws the shirts over them and
they are turned into six swans. Thinking that there are no
more children, she goes home quite happy.

But the sister, who had not run out to meet her, decides to
go and look for her brothers and redeem them. After a long
journey, she finds them and they tell her that they are only
allowed to regain human form for a quarter of an hour every
evening. They say that the only way for her to redeem them
would be if she were to remain dumb for six years, during
which time she would have to make six shirts for them out of
star flowers. The girl decides she will do this and climbs up
a tree and sets to work. But some hunters come and get her

94

down and take her to the king who marries her. The mother-in-law accuses her of killing and eating her children as they are born, and after the third child disappears (taken, as were the others, by the old queen), she is condemned to be burnt as a witch. But the six years are just up and she has finished the shirts, all but one sleeve. Just as the fire is about to be lit the swans appear. As she has brought the shirts with her, she throws them over the birds, who are immediately transformed into men—though the youngest brother has a swan's wing instead of an arm. So the truth comes out. The king is told that his queen is not a witch, the wicked mother is burnt, and the rest of them live together happily.

You see how important it is to study the three stories, which are all variations of the same theme, an amplification of the shirt motif. The shirts can be either the means of bewitchment or of redemption. Hitherto it was necessary for the person to be stripped naked, but in the last story redemption is brought about by putting on the shirt. We have to ask ourselves what that could mean. You have not to get at the naked truth, but to give it a covering to enable it to appear in its true form. A star flower shirt has to be provided, and throwing it over the bewitched person is the redeeming gesture. Here too there is the same motif of long and loving devotion and of great sacrifice.

Projection acts on people like a spell. If you expect the best you are likely to get it, and if you anticipate the worst people are unable to bring out their best: This is something quite essential in the field of education, for if children feel that they are given credit and expected to be able to do something, this has a supporting effect and they can bring out their better side. Here we come to a very subtle problem and one which has caused many errors.

I should like to refer you to Dr. Jung's remarks on projection in *Psychological Types,* where he speaks of the layers of

95

archaic identity.* In writing of these large areas of unconscious identity, Jung says that only if a necessity has arisen
to dissolve the identity can one begin to speak of projection,
but not before. Projection, he says, is first based on archaic
identity. Human beings are all connected and partly identical.
There is no such thing as a completely separated personality.
If Switzerland were attacked, for instance, we should act as
one person. On the layers of the collective unconscious we
are identical with the group. You will find again and again
that Jungian psychologists say that a primitive tribe projects
the Self onto the chief, but this is not correct. What can be
said is that the tribe is in a state of identity in which the chief
is a representative of the Self.

Again, if you meet someone and have the experience of being one heart and one soul—that something has clicked—you
may be sure the other will like what you do. You have a great
identity. But then you ask the final question and are furious
when the other is not one with you, for if you have so much
in common why should he show a difference! Then you have
to realize the projection. At first, however, when there is a
natural harmony of identity, it is not right to speak of it as a
projection, for in projection there is always the idea that something of mine has been ascribed to the other person.

What I project I have never made my own; that is in the
archaic area and that can project itself onto someone else. As
long as there is a "click" you cannot speak of projection because there is a fact, a truth. If your shadow lies, and you
meet another person who also lies, who can prove a projection?
It is the truth. But if my shadow lies and I accuse another person of lying and she does not, there is a malaise, a discomfort,
something does *not* click. One has a bad conscience, one part
of the personality does not believe it any more, and then you
can say that you have projected something. Wrong assumptions

*Collected Works, Vol. 6, par. 783.

have been made which do not correspond with the truth, but only when that phase of disharmony has arisen can one speak of projection. Hitherto there was an archaic identity where one could not make assumptions as to what belonged to the other person, for it was really an interpersonal phenomenon.

The shirt rather represents a mode of self-expression, but I can throw the wrong kind of assumption onto someone and thus bring out the worst in a person. It is important to give credit to the other human being. Some people have a kind of negative expectation everywhere and this brings the worst out of others. It often has a magical effect on very unconscious people who do not know much of such mechanisms; thus it is possible to make them behave badly.

Someone with a negative mother complex, for instance, can play the role so well that every mother figure around is forced into behaving negatively; or a man may have a negative father complex and be against every kind of authority, because for him the father represents traditional authority and everything that smells of that acts like a red rag to a bull. He may behave towards the major on military service in such a way that that officer is forced into asserting authority and power, and is then as much caught in the complex as the other, and has to act out his part. There is a complex which belongs to both which links them together and they have to play it out with each other, though they had never meant to do so. If either has not the same complex, then he will not fall into the trap, but if somewhere in his psyche he has a similar one, then there can be identity. If you listen to either of the two you cannot see the light. But perhaps the more differentiated will tire of the situation and take a stand on his own. He may begin to reflect and decide that even if the other person is as bad as he thinks, he is not going to waste his energy in quarelling any longer for it would be more useful to observe himself. He thus cuts the archaic identity and begins to take back his projection. He will watch his own fantasies and study the com-

97

plex and gradually be no longer caught, but begin to be really free. You can say that he is taking back into his own psychological system what belongs to him, leaving the other alone with his problem.

As soon as there is a tendency for self-reflection and doubt, then projection is there, and not before, even though, as seen by a third person, it looks like it. Contents rarely break through to consciousness directly, though they sometimes may if the conscious attitude is open enough. If you are consciously open to the influx of new contents, the unconscious content can turn up in a dream and through the dream life be brought to consciousness without any outer drama. But even in such a case, especially if the contents are very deep and have many facets, part appears in the interpersonal realm between people. That occurs also with creative intuitions when two people have the same idea at the same moment, as has happened where two or three scientists have independently and simultaneously made the same discovery. The archetypal content does not then belong quite to one or the other and may appear in the interpersonal realm.

When something is pressing towards the threshold of consciousness, you have this interpersonal manifestation which creates first identity and then the realization of projection. That is why these processes first bring people together and then separate them; that is the great régisseur of all positive and negative human dramas. Someone may feel another's soul is akin, but then the two quarrel and the whole *comédie humaine* is started. As long as there is no discomfort or disagreeable feeling, nobody can convince the other person of projection. That is how the flow of life goes and it is not wise to intervene until the person asks why he always quarrels with men or women of a certain type. What belongs to him in that? As long as the thing works, if two people love each other, why for instance should you say that it is only a projection? But when it gets disagreeable, when one feels that something is not working any more, then archaic identity is approaching the state where it can be called a projection.

I would say that the throwing of the shirt is more on the level of archaic identity, and that those interpersonal complexes which affect each other are not yet on the projection level. It seems to me that the different unconscious complexes of the collective unconscious also have a kind of chemical affinity with each other, they affect each other positively or negatively; i.e., certain complexes can hurt other complexes within the unconscious. If we think of ourselves as being the originators of bewitchment and psychological tendencies, then it seems likely that there are contradictory tendencies which affect each other negatively and bring out the worst in others, and only through the interference of consciousness, by finding ways of expression, can you change that. I would interpret the shirt as inadequate, or adequate, fantasy material. Suppose you have an activated, unconscious content within you which is experienced as something restless or stirring and which induces neurotic restlessness. To make such a content conscious, it is tremendously important that it should be provided with adequate means of expression.

I have an analysand, a young girl who, due to a negative mother complex and a difficult father, has practically no feminine ego. She is therefore the playball of everything that happens in her surroundings. If the neighbour says she is horrible, she is completely miserable, and if someone tells her she is pretty, she is on top of the world. She is entirely dependent on others and never really knows what she wants or who she really is. On account of her weak ego she is always frightened of bringing out a negative reaction in the other person, for she would not be able to stand it; so she gives the impression of being very false. She never says anything negative but thanks you for everything. You have the feeling that there is a lot of criticism behind, but she always avoids awkward reactions. Actually, when the negative side does appear she indulges

99

in a lot of negative gossiping. Human gossip always reaches the ears of the wrong person!

When she came to analysis she was quite wild. People used to think she was an intriguer, and she lost just what she wanted, human contact. In analysis she treated me as the superior and had no courage to admit negative feelings, she said she could not bring them out. She bottled up a tremendous amount of rage against her surroundings but never expressed it. She had heard of active imagination and had read about it in Jung's books and she began to do what turned out to be black magic. She imagined the person she hated and called it abreacting her rage in order to overcome it, while actually she was getting worse and worse. I saw from a dream that she was practising black magic and accused her of it and then discovered what she was doing. I told her that she must never deal with another person's, but with her own rage, that she should observe herself and ask what *she* was doing with her own shadow. You have to leave out the other person on whom the rage falls; that is the difference between black magic and active imagination. You have to put the right exorcising shirt on your own affect!

When there is a question of redeeming someone, i.e., a part of one's own psyche, it is always a question of giving him the right kind of expression, the right kind of fantasy material within which he can express himself.

Lecture 7

Last time we discussed the problem of the seven ravens and the six swans in the fairytales. In the story of the six swans the girl has to make shirts from star flowers, little flowers which grow in the dark in the woods and which, since they are like little white stars, are looked upon in folklore as the stars of Heaven growing on earth. From these the girl makes the shirts which she throws over her brothers, who thereby become human. We considered how far this is connected with projection, or with providing the unconscious complex with an appropriate expression through fantasy material. I think especially of the technique of active imagination, which we try to use when a very dynamic content of the unconscious is constellated and disturbing consciousness, provided that certain conditions are fulfilled—i.e., that the ego is not too weak and that there is no psychosis, for one must be very careful with this technique.

Under the right conditions, we try to allow this complex of the unconscious to express itself in fantasy while we participate consciously. In this way the material amplifies itself in a different way from in the dream. Every dream is an amplification of an unconscious content, while in active imagination there is active conscious cooperation, a conscious effort, which influences the material on one side, but which also adds to it certain factors, and in this cooperation of conscious and unconscious a transforming process can take place.

There are people who pretend that they can influence their dreams, but I have never found that they could. Sometimes you have the experience in a dream of thinking that you don't want to dream that, and then you wake up, but this is a fear reaction by which you repress. You cannot alter dreams. The

101

only way we know of influencing the unconscious is by the technique of active imagination. It is true that other things do have an influence, but a repressive one. In the *exercitia spiritualia* of Ignatius of Loyola, a particular subject is given for meditation, there is a definite plan of procedure. This applies also for most of the yoga practices, as far as we know. They say, for instance, that at a certain stage beautiful Devas will appear and try to lure you, but you must resist the temptation; or there are rules by which concentration has to be kept fixed.

In contrast to these practices we take the attitude that in such a dialectic process, in which the conscious and unconscious confront each other, ego consciousness has to determine each time what it wants, without advance programming. If in a man's imagination a beautiful goddess tries to lure him away, he can decide to follow her or not—there is no rule. At each step the decision lies with the conscious, as it would in life. That makes a tremendous difference. If this technique is practised properly, there is to a certain extent the possibility of influencing the unconscious, and one can experience a great release from the tension due to the obsessive force of an unconscious content. It is also a good way in which to work out certain affects, or to bring up unconscious creative material which is difficult to understand or cannot appear in some already existing material; for we give the unconscious a chance to express itself while adding the focussing and concentrating elements of consciousness, so that the product is that of the two worlds in an in-between sphere, which we call the reality of the psyche.

That, I think, is what could be compared to the star flower shirt in our fairytale. The girl makes a long and devoted effort to give the swans a form by which they can return to human shape, and that is similar to the process of active imagination: we take a human standpoint towards unconscious contents, we talk to them as if they were human beings, which has a mystically humanizing effect and gives to the animus or anima, for instance, a mode of expression.

102

Every content of the unconscious with which one is not properly related tends to obsess one for it gets at us from behind. If you can talk to it you get into relationship with it. You can either be possessed by a content constellated in the unconscious, or you can have a relationship to it. The more one suppresses it, the more one is affected by it. If we don't actively offer the unconscious a means of expression, it comes out in destructive, undermining, involuntary fantasy material.

People who are possessed and spun up in a cocoon about the people they ought to relate to are caught in the most amazing assumptions, which they neither doubt nor make quite clear to themselves because they seem to be completely evident. They are sure of everything and never say, "Why do I assume such a thing?" The obsession becomes a complete semi-conscious conviction. That happens when fantasy material has found a wrong mode of expression, e.g., in accusations against neighbours and friends, and it is never checked. It skulks at the back of the mind of such a person and amplifies itself. Little irrelevant instances are picked up and built into a paranoic system and every item adds a bit more—e.g., the Swiss Government has decided so and so, or the postman's ring means this or that—everything is one more sign. Even the minds of so-called normal people are filled with unchecked assumptions which are not related to conscious reality. If you ask them about this you will meet a completely erratic block and discover a crazy idea. There the technique of active imagination is proper. You have to put the idea or hunch in front of you and talk to it. When you have overcome a certain cramp of consciousness and the doubt in your mind that you are making it up, you can provide the content with a possibility of expressing itself in fantasy; this requires an objective attitude towards one's own material.

The girl, while making these star flower shirts, must also not speak a word, a theme which appears in other variations too, and she gets accused of killing her children and being bewitched, etc. This is another redemption motif. Not to speak would mean not to have any connection with the people around you, and not to discuss the problem. Here there is an element which occurs naturally very frequently, namely that you are overwhelmed by something which takes away your capacity for speech. In catatonic states there is no capacity for speech, the emotions induced by the problem are overwhelming and speech is impossible. In minor cases, when you are deeply moved by something you cannot talk, for there is again the opposition between what happens involuntarily and what happens when you add an effort to it. If such a content tends to make you speechless, it is better to add to it by making up your mind not to talk of it. If you add a conscious effort, or attitude, then the rather destructive or dangerous element becomes positive.

So, if you are overwhelmed by an unconscious content and cannot speak of it, then do not try to talk about it in the outer world but let it first express itself to you. Then you are not overwhelmed by unknown emotion, which is always a dynamic fact flowing towards something. The *primitive* unconscious impulse would be to follow that secret tendency of the emotion where it wants to lead. If it is hate, it carries you involuntarily towards the hated object; if it is love, it is the same thing, to mention only two common emotions. If you try to express the emotion first toward its object, there is great danger of being overwhelmed. Say someone is furious but intends to express the fact decently, yet with one word comes the flow, and though one may have determined to say little, the whole avalanche descends! In the moment of affect one says much more and gets more and more involved, and in the end one believes what one doubted at the beginning.

If active imagination is practised by unsuitable people, the fantasy is expressed in the way they feel their own material, but their emotion gets stronger and stronger and in the end leads to catastrophe, for the affect has increased on the way. One must first weave the material for the shirt, find a way of self-expression, and then let the emotion out in its own place. A Jesuit of the 17th century said the human tongue is like a fiery wheel, it spreads poisonous fire and destruction everywhere. The negative aspect is quite devilish. Think of the propaganda in our days and what can be done by it, even murder.

People who write articles full of hatred in the papers would be wiser to keep quiet and work on their affect—that would be giving the man a shirt so that the emotion could come out in human shape. The same thing also occurs constantly in analysis. The way in which resistance is expressed makes all the difference in the world. If it is just thrown out, it demands a lot of the analyst not to get emotional too. But if the analysand says that in the last hour he felt a certain resistance and would like to discuss this and that point, then there is a normal human situation—for the thing has been presented in the right shirt.

Unfortunately, possession carries the conviction that one is right. Just as Russian protagonists are convinced that the Western world is the destructive thing, so if the animus has you, you are sure that it is so. The great thing is to know that. Like most of my brothers and sisters, when I am possessed by the animus, I do not notice it—I am convinced it is my own and not the animus's opinion. But if you have analysed for a while, you know from the tone of the voice and the intensity of the emotion that something is not right. There is too much drive behind what you want to have, or do, and that is suspect. You have the feeling that you have heard that kind of argument before within yourself. When you are too much in the animus you cannot get out of it at once, so keep quiet. Go back into your room and say, "This is all wrong, there is something very suspicious about the state in which I find myself so I will not say anything for a few days," and then afterwards you can thank God that for once you managed to keep it inside. But it might fester and get worse and that is where you

105

need the shirt; you must not just keep it back and be poisoned and let it worm around inside you, for that does not help. If poison festers inside it may get worse after three days, but if within that time you give it a shirt, say in active imagination, then you can avoid trouble.

I have alluded to the case of the girl who was always so nice and polite because she wanted to be loved, and then piled up hate against a married man. The couple whom she sometimes met had the same disease, so naturally they accused each other of being false and dishonest. Once when she had been to their home for lunch she came back in a pathological rage against the man who was false and a liar—an awful person behind a sweet mask. She had not said anything. It would not have been better if she had, she would have let out too much, so it piled up and when she got to her room she could not work or concentrate because the thing was raging in her. In her fantasy material she just gave vent to her rage by fantasying what she would do to the man, namely hang him, spit at him, etc. A dream then said that she had fallen into witchcraft and black magic. I accused her of this but she could not think of anything she had done, so I went through all that had taken place during the last days and it came out about the fantasies. I told her that if the affect disturbed her to such an extent she must personify it, but not by the person concerned—rather as a raging bear, or as a creature which tries to smash up things. If you just give rein to the affect and deal with the wrong fantasies which come up, that increases the *abaissement du niveau mental*. Holding one's tongue, keeping the affect within and then giving it an appropriate means of expression, is the proper course in this redemption motif.

We can just as well take a completely different content. Say that suddenly, like a raven or a swan flying across the sky, you have a megalomanic idea, in some way you are the godhead itself. You may say this is nonsense, or you may nurse the idea, but don't speak of it for others would not believe it. You

106

have not made up the fantasy, but you might ask how it came into your head. Of course it came by itself! If you go about saying that you are the godhead, people will know where to put you, but if you keep it to yourself and ask yourself how you got that idea you can discover most amazing material. Then, like the mystics, you find that in every human being there is a divine spark and your personality is increased by an inner experience, though the first appearance of it was very shocking. So one needs to sit up in a tree, so to speak, and be completely detached; let the thing express itself by adding a lot of devotion to the material instead of letting oneself be overwhelmed by it.

Paracelsus said that every human was a cosmos with all the stars within himself. The starry sky is an image of the collective unconscious, and if the stars come down to the earth that carries the symbolism of realization, for the thing becomes real within the consciousness of the human being. What is not realized is not real. Before the atom was realized, it existed, though it was not in human consciousness. The stars come down from Heaven and are woven into the shirt and thus realized in an archetypal pattern. The one wing left would mean that integration, becoming conscious, is a very relative thing. As Goethe said: *"Uns bleibt ein Endenrest, zu tragen peinlich."* (There is left to us a remnant, difficult to carry.) The same is true for an archetypal content, which cannot be integrated entirely. The meaning of the symbol can be exhausted for one's subjective feeling, but one has not exhausted the whole meaning. I take fairytales and interpret them until I feel at peace in my own mind, but I don't feel that I have exhausted the material. If I have not done enough, I feel uncomfortable, then I generally have dreams and know that my unconscious is not yet satisfied with my interpretation, but it is a purely relative thing. Sometimes people think if you analysed for twenty years, the unconscious would be exhausted, but practically it never is, there are always more aspects, as though it had the ability to go on creating. There is always the one wing which reaches back into the unknown.

One amazing fact is that when the girl is with the seven ravens, there are eight altogether, the number of totality; and in the story of the six swans, when the girl marries there are again eight. At the end of both fairytales you have eight persons. The symbolism of this motif is discussed by Jung in *Psychology and Alchemy,** where the difficult step from three to four, or seven to eight, is related to the problem of integrating the fourth, inferior function. Here there is always a great difficulty, which has to do with the fact that the unconscious cannot be completely integrated and the fourth function always remains more or less autonomous. This is actually a good thing, for it means that the flow of life goes on and always constellates new material and new problems. The whole is never integrated, and supposing it could be, it would mean the petrification of the life process.

The next motif could be called the Amor and Psyche motif, which is taken from *The Golden Ass,* a late antique, second century novel by Apuleius. It is the story of a man who studied witchcraft in Thessaly and wished to find out about the secret witchcraft practised by his hostess. But things go wrong and he gets changed into an ass, though he could return to his own shape if he could eat roses. At the end of the story he discovers a priest carrying a bunch of red roses, in a procession of initiates into the Isis and Osiris mysteries, and at last he is able to resume his human shape and be initiated into these mysteries. During the time that he was an ass, he was also used as a pack animal by robbers and had to carry loads for them. The robbers had stolen a girl at a wedding, and while the men were eating, an old woman told the girl, who was crying, the fairy story which is often published separately.

---

*Collected Works, Vol. 12, pars. 201ff.

Erich Neumann, in *Amor and Psyche,* has interpreted this tale from the angle of feminine psychology, but it is really more concerned with the man's anima, and anima psychology. Apuleius wrote it as a folk tale, which he inserted into his novel at the right place, for the story itself had existed long before his time. What is interesting is that in German and Nordic mythology you find parallel motifs quite independent from our story, which shows how widespread these motifs are.

In the antique version, a royal princess, Psyche, is seduced by the son of the goddess Venus, the god Eros, or Amor, who lives with her in a palace where invisible servants bring the food. She never sees her husband; he is invisible, but he sleeps with her at night without her ever knowing with whom she is living. Her two sisters poison her with suspicion, telling her that she is married to a dragon who only makes love to her and feeds her well in order to eat her in the end. The suspicion grows, and the devilish sisters advise her to take an oil lamp and a knife, to hide them and look at her husband in the night and kill the dragon. When she lights the lamp she sees a most beautiful winged youth, but a drop of burning oil from the lamp falls on him. He awakes and says he had not wanted her to know about him and to punish her he flies away, leaving her alone. She wants to kill herself, but decides to look for him and sets out on a long quest.

In this case it is not the light of the lamp, but the burning oil which makes the partner visible, wounding him so that he disappears and is lost. There is an equivalent German fairytale, "The Three Black Princesses," where the redemption motif is different. A young man goes into a black castle in the woods and finds three black princesses buried to the waist in the earth. He asks if he can redeem them. They say that he can if he does not speak for a year and tells nobody about them or what he is doing, but if he gives away the secret the brothers of the princesses will kill him. For a while he keeps his promise, but

when at home his mother keeps asking him why he does not
speak and he grows weak and tells her. She thinks there is
something very uncanny about it and says he should take a
candle from the church and some holy water, and when he
goes back he should light the candle and sprinkle the water. He
does so, and the princesses become white as far as the waist
and say that if only he had kept his promise he would have redeemed them, but now nobody will ever be able to do it and
their brothers will kill him. He takes a chance and jumps out
the window; he breaks his leg and the castle disappears and he
remains a cripple. In this case it is an anima figure which is
destroyed by the bringing of the light.

Another variation appears in Grimm's "The Singing, Soaring
Lark." A rich businessman has three daughters. He asks them
what he should bring them when he comes back from a journey.
One asks for pearls, the second for diamonds, and the third
says she wants a singing, soaring lark. He cannot find what his
youngest daughter wants, until on the way home he sees a
lark on a tree in the woods; but it is guarded by a lion which
says that he can only have the bird if he, the lion, may marry
the girl. The lion frightens the man so badly that he goes home
and tells his daughter, but she agrees and lives with the lion in
a castle. Every night he sheds his skin and becomes a beautiful
prince, but in the daytime he is a lion. After a time she gets
homesick and wants to see her sisters. The lion warns her, but
there is to be a wedding feast for one of the sisters and she insists that he should accompany her to it. He says that if any
light falls on him there will be disaster, so the girl arranges
that he shall be kept shut up in a room without light. But
there is a crack in one of the walls and a little light filters
through and when it falls on him he is turned into a dove.
When she comes to see the lion she finds only the dove, who
tells her that now he has to fly among doves for seven years,
but that if she wants to follow him she can do so, for with
every seventh step he will let a drop of blood and a white

110

feather fall. The girl then has to go on a long and painful quest to find him at the end of the world beyond the Red Sea and a terrible wood and there redeem him.

Here again it is the light which is destructive, but there are also the girl's sisters. In other versions, the partner disappears when he is called by his animal name, or if anything about him is betrayed to the sisters, but I want to concentrate on versions which have the light motif in them. This motif is most surprising because we are accustomed to think that light in general is only positive. Light is a symbol for consciousness; we get enlightened, and we talk about the light of consciousness falling on someone, etc. Here there is a kind of mystical union between two loving partners which is fed by mystery. It is a union which takes place in the night and is not touched by any driven light of consciousness, but the moment light falls on it there is separation and suffering and perhaps even definite destruction of the possibility of redemption, like the crippling of the man who should have redeemed the three black princesses.

This would point to a destructiveness of consciousness, namely that to certain contents of the unconscious the light of consciousness is not positive but destructive. That is something that all analysts and future analysts should realize to the full extent. It is an archetypal motif, which means that it is most widespread and important. Consciousness is destructive and causes separation within a certain realm which is clearly characterized as the realm of Eros. It is here that the light of consciousness can have a completely destructive effect. One has the feeling also, from the way the light disappears, that if the girl could have held on to the mystery and gone on with it indefinitely, then some redemption would at some time have taken place.

Naturally, the intrusion of the light has to do with the fact that it was brought in too soon. Some of the disappearing animals have said this, and that in consequence the partner

111

would have to make a long effort to find the other again, so the motif of right timing comes in once more. Here the partner is either an animal or not just an animal, but a god, and Psyche, for instance, naturally has a suspicion that he might be a dragon, as the sisters have suggested. What she discovers is that she is married to the most beautiful divine figure, which is typical, for the divine and the animal are very close to each other.

The divine is either above or below the human level, it makes no difference. In one situation the mysterious husband is above human level and in another the mystery is that he is below. The alchemists say that above is below, i.e., the animal is identical with the divine principle. This mystery of being above or below the human level has to do with its being touchy about being seen in the light of consciousness, for that can destroy such elements of what is above or below and not recognized in its own realm. It is the light of consciousness contained in the sphere of the sisters or the realm of the mother which is destructive, for they are the negative, jealous females around.

The destructive light is that which comes from the wedding of one of the sisters, or is thrown on the god at the suggestion of one of them; or, in the story of the black princesses, the mother of the hero suggests that he should take a light, and that has to do with the danger of jealous or malevolent feelings. It is not the hero's own decision, but an independent one. But in the case of the lion-lark there is no decision, the girl only suggests that he should come to the wedding feast, which shows a wrong "drive" on her part. Those who want to be redeemed always shun the light for it has a destructive effect on embryonic contents or those in a state of transformation. If you change the place of a plant and suddenly put it into the sunlight, it will collapse, just as sunlight can destroy us if we expose ourselves too much to it, if we are too long in it. In both stories light is brought in for negative or malicious reasons, for the wrong motive.

112

If you take it on the psychological level, you can say that in this light of recognition there is a nuance of a "nothing but" attitude. It makes a world of difference if I say "this is this" or if I say it is "nothing but this." If something is in a growing process and I say, "It is *this*," then it can still change, but if I say it is "nothing but," this attitude limits and stops transformation and the possibility of further growth. If the intellect does not say, "It appears to me that way," but is accompanied by that subtle psychological attitude which says, "I know it is just this and not more," then the "nothing but" nuance brings in what is devilish or Luciferian and destroys everything, especially the growing thing. What is already petrified is no longer important. If I think in this way of a railway, that is not harmed, but if I think I know all about plant life and that it is only this and that chemical process, then I block off any possibility of saying more.

All contents of the soul have to come back to the other motif of the swan wing—they all have an aspect which is not yet recognized. The philosophical system with which we try to interpret contents of the unconscious is open to still more, and that is the way in which an interpretation will not have a destructive effect. One should keep to what is possible and infer at the same time that there is a lot more to it so that there is room for growth.

The light of the Church would not have destroyed the princesses but for the malevolent commands of the mother of the hero, which would mean that the motive with which it was used was wrong. The mother was entirely hostile to his future bride. It was not due to the holy water itself that it worked negatively, but because the mother brought in a negative element. Holy water and candlelight are used for exorcism, so when she says he should take holy water she implies that the princesses are evil and "nothing but" witches—she brings in a nuance which is not in the story itself, for they wanted to become white and were not witches. In sprinkling holy water over them the hero expresses the thought that they are probably "nothing but" witches and thereby destroys his own soul.

Everything which is malevolent or profane always results in giving the thing that "nothing but" attitude. In intellectual discussions there are people who seem to want the last word; there is a sharp kind of drive in their argument which is not necessary in an intellectual formulation. When not used as an instrument, the intellect becomes autonomous and dynamic and one can be sure that a man with such an attitude is driven by his anima, otherwise he would discuss in a quiet, detached way. There may be a certain supplementary aspect which has not been seen as yet. Scientists of the nineteenth century always claimed to show the absolute truth; they had the idea of "now we know" and not the kind of open attitude of modern scientists, who say: "What we observe leads us to this conclusion." This leaves the thing open for whatever decisions may be reached, there is always the idea not of the absolute truth, but only of a relative truth.

This would be an example of the necessary change in attitude, to the awareness that the intellect is an instrument with which we can "light up" certain realms, but by which we also shut out other aspects. That is true most certainly in the interpretation of psychological material: if we describe it from one angle we could say that it appears to shed a meaningful light on the material from that aspect, but that there are a thousand more things which might be discovered.

The arrogant intellectual attitude generally comes from unconscious motives such as prestige, or power drives, or fear defence mechanisms. The intellect should be purified of false motives and its instrumental quality should not be forgotten. The instrumental factor should be used by the whole personality and not be the autonomous thing which is picked up by unconscious motives of fear or policy, etc., for these poison the reflecting instrument.

The case of the black princesses describes the mother's destructive motive. In the case of the lion-lark, we cannot prove any psychological attitude but we know that the two sisters wanted jewellery, which showed a worldly and set attitude towards life, and possibly this had to do with the fact that the light from the wedding feast destroyed something in the youngest sister's wedding—the worldly or driven motive falling onto something absolutely mystical in character. This throws a lot of light on feminine psychology where it is very difficult to separate love from social motivations, because the love situation with a woman and her social status have historically always been combined. In the Islamic world, for instance, the woman becomes a member of a harem. The state of marriage for a woman is usually combined with her prestige and social life and this prestige always poisons the pure feeling attitude.

With the anima of a man it is different, in so far as his Eros is partly given to his beloved profession, the ideas he loves, or the field of spiritual experience he lives, which brings in the worldly motive. Many men have given up investigation in certain fields because they could not make a career out of it; a man defeats the inner experience if he puts his spiritual cognition more into the service of his career, so betraying his instinct for the truth, for then the "jewellery" poisons the atmosphere of the mystical inner marriage within his soul.

The situation may not always be destroyed completely; in the story of the black princesses the man is definitely crippled, but in other stories a long journey has to be taken to find the loved one again. That happens when people succumb to the power or prestige drive and lose their oneness with themselves—until the unhappiness and discomfort which ensue force them to go in search of the soul again. It is then generally a long process of seeking, and of giving up the worldly advantages one had at first in order to find the inner wholeness again; or the partner may be redeemed by suffering or by a kiss given the ugly toad (redemption by overcoming repulsion).

Now I want to touch on one more motif and that is the

115

cutting off of the head. In some fairytales there is a helpful animal who comes to the aid of the hero or heroine—he gives them advice or helps them and foretells the dangers. Sometimes one of the two, the bride or bridegroom, is turned into an animal who at the end of the story asks to be beheaded. Generally the one who should do this refuses, saying that he owes it too much, but the animal insists; or there is an intermission after which it returns, and at last the hero makes up his mind and pulls out his sword and beheads it and out comes a human being who had been changed by a curse into animal form.

Grimm's story of "The Golden Bird" tells of a hero who has to find a beautiful princess; he is helped by a fox who in the end says, "You must cut off my head and feet." The hero refuses, for he cannot be so ungrateful, but the fox meets him again and once more begs him to cut off his head and feet; this time the hero does and there appears a beautiful prince, the brother of the princess and the brother-in-law of the hero, who in order to regain human form had to be beheaded.

Then there is the German fairytale where the boy finds an enchanted castle and a little black dog who asks to be beheaded, and when this takes place the castle is redeemed and the dog turns into a princess.

In another of Grimm's fairytales, "The White Bride and the Black Bride," a witch has two daughters, one of whom is a witch like herself, and the other, a stepdaughter, who is beautiful and good. There is also a stepson through whom his sister gets into touch with the king who wants to marry her. They all set out in a carriage for the Court. On the way, the witch mother insists that her stepdaughter shall give her clothes to the witch's own daughter. When this is done they push the stepdaughter into a river; she is turned into a duck and it is the witch sister who marries the king. From time to time the duck goes into the royal kitchen and says a little verse which shows what happened. The kitchen boy listens and tells the king

116

about the strange duck. The king comes to see it and when the duck appears he cuts off its head and there is the beautiful princess. She then becomes the queen and the witch and stepsister are punished.

Here the animal has to be beheaded. We are focussing our attention on the theme of the beheading, but cutting off a human being's head is a very widespread motif in alchemy where it has to do with the separation of the intellect from the instinctual aspect. In *Mysterium Conjunctionis,* Jung speaks of the beheading of the dragon and of the Ethiopian and interprets this as the separation of the intellect from the more instinctual aspect of the psyche.* There it would mean two things: namely, if you separate the intellect from the instinctive drives there results a certain mental detachment or objectivity, so that one can look at one's own material—drives, impulses, and thoughts—without prejudice. The intellect separates itself from the unconscious connection with the rest of the personality and becomes a purely mirroring detached factor, as you can observe in active imagination where detachment linked with courage is required. One has to detach from one's ego and look objectively.

But beheading can also mean a *sacrificium intellectus,* a giving up of the wish to understand in order to let certain other forms of realization take place. If I am constantly *thinking* about a relationship, I can inhibit the possibility of a feeling realization, and therefore the intellect sometimes has to detach and to let other forms of life come up. For the divine mystery one has to give up the narrow wish of only intellectual understanding, and where other forms of realization should come about in the soul the intellect should take a back place for a while and keep to its own realm of operation.

It is different if you behead an animal, because in an animal the head would be relatively the more intellectual part of the

---

*Collected Works, Vol. 14, pars. 730f.

body. We are generally inclined to project consciousness and thinking into the head of a being. To behead an animal would mean to separate its intelligence from its body, which definitely gives the whole thing a different aspect from the beheading of a human being, for it would mean to cut off that element in the drive which consists in cunning planning. Animals do not go so far as to build up a philosophical system, at least we do not know that they do, but we do know that their intelligence appears like cunning planning, or the use of certain actions with a definite aim; we do not know whether this is done consciously or unconsciously, but we can observe from the outside that the animal has behaved intelligently. This can be watched in animal drives in a human being. In feminine psychology it is expressed in plotting or intriguing—all the semi-conscious intriguing a woman can indulge in, such as sitting at a lecture "by chance" beside a man in whom she is interested, and so on. Her instinctive drive does not coincide with her ego consciousness. You find this just as much in the shadow and anima of men. Our drives have a tendency to produce planned actions for the achievement of their objectives and these disturb the conscious oneness of the personality: the right hand does not know what the left hand does, an impure element has been introduced.

St. Thomas Aquinas speaks of the difference between *concupiscentia* and *cupiditas,* the former being just a natural drive when you want something—the fleshly part of man which drives him. But in cupidity, greed or some such intellectual quality is added and gives the drive an additional impure, devilish aspect, introducing the element of planning or cunning. You can compare the behaviour of a driven human being with that of an animal. The animal has its own tricks, or another drive can cross the first, and so on. But in a human being something combined with a certain amount of consciousness can intervene, thereby intensifying the urge, for something has got in which did not originally belong and the instinctual

118

realm is poisoned and not functioning in its right way. By separating and cutting out the element which belongs to human consciousness, and leaving the body of the animal which is the raw material of the instinctual drive, the whole problem can be integrated at a human level.

I want to add a final word. You have probably noticed that I have used another way of thinking in interpreting all these tales. When one has to do with such symbolic folklore one can think in one of two ways: one can think about it, or one can put oneself outside, above, or beside the material and have thoughts about it and see if they fit. You cannot get out of the first way, it is the traditional way of thinking learnt in school. But when one has practised the other way for a while, one's thinking gets altered; one does not stop to think about it, the thinking process is rather like listening to what the symbol itself has to say. Then thinking becomes an instrument which lends itself to self-expression of the material.

That is what Jung calls *symbolic thinking*. It is something difficult to learn and the more one has learnt the scholarly way, the more difficult it is to switch to this symbolic thinking. But through it you have an invaluable instrument for understanding the raw material of the psyche and its new and not yet known expressions, which we have to know if we want to deal with the unconscious. I would encourage you to make an effort in this direction, for it can bring out of otherwise unintelligible material a new light and wealth of understanding.

Index

active imagination, 43, 69, 99-107, 117
affect, *see* motion
Aion (Jung), 84
albedo, 39, 75
alchemy: 23, 30; *albedo*, 39, 75;
  animals in, 112; beheading in, 117;
  extractio animae, 89; hermaphrodite in, 78; king in, 83-84; *nigredo*,
  38-39, 75; projection in, 89; verdigris in, 71; vessel in, 28-29
alienation, from instincts, 17, 21, 38-
  39, 53-54, 118-119
Amor and Psyche, 108-109
amplification, 25-26, 31, 101-102
analysis: as bathing, 9, 24-25, 36; demands in, 86: and electric shock,
  56-57, 65; emotion in, 64-67, 105;
  resistance in, 105
Andersen, Hans Christian, 90
anima: 10-11, 25, 39; as animal, 57,
  80; bewitched, 39-48, 67-69, 70-
  74; as black dog, 39-40, 42-43;
  contaminated by male complex,
  41-42, 73-74; dialogue with, 102;
  as dragon skin, 80; as frog princess,
  60-63, 67, 70-73; lover of, 41;
  moods, 39-40; neurotic, 17; as
  pagan, 40-41, 43-44; projection of,
  71, 81; as Psyche, 108-109; and
  sexuality, 43-46; as Virgin Mary,
  81; and *Weltanschauung*, 40-48;
  and wizard, 40-43, 48, 73
animal skins: burning of, 62-67, 73;
  over human, 8, 42, 66, 77, 116-
  119
animals: beheading of, 116-119; bewitched, 7, 17, 22-23, 37-40, 43,
  48, 53, 57-58, 60-63, 70, 110-112,
  116-119; as divine principle, 112;
  doctor, 58; helpful, 13, 19, 116;
  pattern of behaviour, 20-21, 37-
  39, 49-51; speaking, 12, 116
animus: 18; possession by, 105; projection of, 71
Anthropos, 80
Apocalypse, 90
Apuleius, 37, 91, 108-109

aqua doctrinae, 32
aqua ignita, 36
archaic identity, 96-99
archetypes: 9-16, 19-21; and image,
  49; and instincts, 49, 51-53, 56, 67;
  as ordering spirit, 49, 67
arrogance, 114
arrow, 61, 69-71
asperges, 36
ass, 37-38, 48, 108

Baba Yaga, 61
ball, of flesh, 89
baptism, 17, 23-24, 35-36
bath/bathing: 7-9, 21-25, 29-37, 77,
  83; as amplification, 25; as analytical process, 9, 24-25; in catatonia,
  37; in milk, 7, 22-23, 77, 83; and
  shadow problems, 25; in urine, 22;
  in water, 8, 22-25, 29-31
bathtub, 28-29
bear, 7, 60, 106
beating, 8, 23, 26-27, 77, 83
bees, 49-51
behaviour: patterns of, 20-21, 37-39,
  49-51; "right" kind, 19-20
beheading, 8-9, 22, 39, 116-119
Benedictio Fontis, 35
bewitchment: as alienation from instincts, 17, 21, 53-54; as animal,
  7, 17, 22-23, 37-43, 48, 53, 57-63,
  70, 110-112, 116-119; with animal
  skins, 42, 53, 60, 83; as bird, 50-
  51, 54; and neurosis, 7-8, 16-18,
  25, 53-54; by shirt, 95
birds, 39, 50-51, 54, 116
black magic, 27-28, 100, 106
bleeding flesh, as naked truth, 87-91,
  95
blood, 55
Book of Tobit, 23
bow and arrow, 69-71
Buddha/Buddhism, 79-80, 84
burning: of animal skin, 62-67, 73;
  oil, 109
bush soul, 12

120

candle: in *Amor and Psyche*, 109; Easter, 35-36

castle, *see* palace

Catholic Church: 28, 35-36, 80, 88; as vessel, 28

catatonia, 37, 56-57, 104

children, psychology of, 14-15, 66, 70

Christianity: baptism in, 24; and Self, 80, 88

clothes, 90-91; *see also* shirt

coffin, 27

collective unconscious, 9, 16, 96

complex: and amplification, 25-26, 29; bewitchment of, 16-18; death of, 27; dialogue with, 43-44, 99-107; and drivenness, 39, 42-43, 67, 85-86; father, 26, 97; heating up of, 32-33; interrelation of, 48, 99; mother, 97; possession by, 73-74, 86, 103-105; repression of, 27-28, 62-63, 68-69, 101-103; syphilis, 25-26, 29

"Comrade, The" (Norwegian), 22

concupiscentia, 118

conflict, 30

consciousness: destructive, 109-114; as light, 111-114; union with unconscious, 36, 90, 101-102; as vessel, 28

constellation, of archetypal situation, 12, 101

container, *see* vessel

coolness, as reason, 30-32

copper, 71-72

corpse, dream of, 59-60

Courts of Love, 81

cow, 17

cupiditas, 118

cutting off: the head, *see* beheading; paws, 39, 116

Dead Sea Scrolls, 24

death, projected onto Self, 55

depression, 35, 37-39, 44-45

Dionysus, 38, 44

discrimination, 89-90

dismemberment, 9, 78

doctor animals, 58

dog, 39-40, 42-43, 116

Don Juan, 72

dove, 8, 22, 110-111

dragon, 76-78, 80, 83, 86

dreams: 8, 16, 29, 33, 59, 89-90; amplification of, 25, 101-102; of anima's lover, 41; of animals, 58-59; archetypal, 56-57; of being killed, 34; of coffin, 27; of corpse, 59; of ghosts, 54; influencing, 101-102

drivenness, 39, 42-43, 67, 85-86, 112-119

duck, 7, 116-117

Easter candle, 35-36

eating flowers, 8, 37, 76-77, 80, 108

egg, 31

ego: 10-11, 14-15; contaminated by Self, 78-80, 83; continuity of, 15-16; as hero/heroine, 16, 19-21, 40; identified with Self, 15-16, 78-80; overwhelmed by complex, 39, 42-43; projected, 14; weak, 15; wrong attitude of, 43-47, 73

electric shock therapy, 56-57, 65

Eleusynian mysteries, 23

emotion: in analysis, 64-67; and fire, 36, 64-67; overwhelmed by, 42-43, 104; and water temperature, 30-33

Eros, 26, 109, 111

exercitia spiritualia, 102

extractio animae, 89

fairytales: and myths, 9-13; origin of, 11-13

fairytales, interpreted: The Comrade, 22; The Frog Who Was a Czar's Daughter, 60-63, 67, 70-73, 78; The Golden Bird, 39, 116; King Lindworm, 76-77, 80, 83, 91; King Porco, 62-64; No Chia, 88-89; The Seven Ravens, 17, 93-94; The Singing, Soaring Lark, 110-112; The Six Swans, 42, 94-95; The Three Black Princesses, 109-110; The Twelve Brothers, 91-93; The White Bride and the Black Bride, 116-117

121

122

"Singing, Soaring Lark, The" (Grimm), 110-112
"Six Swans, The" (Grimm), 42, 94-95
skins, animal: 8, 42, 53, 60, 66, 77, 83; burning of, 62-67, 73
snake, 7, 58, 76
spirit: as glass, 75; as order, 49, 67
star: flowers, 94, 101; on forehead, 92
starry sky, as unconscious, 107
suicide, 54-55
swan, 7, 42, 94-95, 102, 106
sweat bath, 22-23
sword, 89-90
symbolic thinking, 29, 119
symptoms, symbolism of, 26-27
synchronicity, 12
syphilis complex, 25-26, 29

Tell, William, 11
temperature, and emotion, 30-33
therapy, *see* analysis
Thérésa of Avila, 73
three, and four, 108
"Three Black Princesses, The" (Grimm), 109-110
tiger, 58-60
timing, of redemption, 60-63, 112-114
toad, kissing, 115
tree, sitting in, 107
troll, 22, 40, 48
trollskin, 22-23
"Twelve Brothers, The" (Grimm), 91-93

unconscious: autonomy of, 59; as bathtub, 28; collective, 9, 16, 96; dialogue with, *see* active imagination; possession by, 78-79, 103-105; relationship with, 103; as starry sky, 107; union with consciousness, 36, 90, 101-102; as water, 24
understanding: as candle light, 35-36; as water, 30-32

van der Post, Laurens, 71
Venus, 71-72, 109
verdigris, 71
vessel, 28-29
Virgin Mary, as anima, 81

washing, *see* bath/bathing
water: baptismal, 35-36; as emotion, 30; and fire, 35-36; heating artificially, 33-34; renewal by, 24; temperature of, 30-37; and understanding, 30-31
weapons, in bride's body, 23
Weltanschauung, problem of, 40-48, 54, 68-69
whipping, *see* beating
"White Bride and the Black Bride, The" (Grimm), 116-117
white garments, 23-24, 91
wing, 107-108, 113
witch soul, as fox, 12-13
wizard, and anima, 40-43, 48, 73
wolf, 7, 58, 60
women's plots, 118

yoga, 102

Zen Buddhism, 79

Studies in Jungian Psychology
by Jungian Analysts

LIMITED EDITION PAPERBACKS

Prices quoted are in U.S. dollars (except for Canadian orders)

1. The Secret Raven: Conflict and Transformation.
Daryl Sharp (Toronto). ISBN 0-919123-00-7. 128 pp. $10
Concise introduction to the application of Jungian psychology. Illustrated.

2. The Psychological Meaning of Redemption Motifs in Fairytales.
Marie-Louise von Franz (Zurich). ISBN 0-919123-01-5. 128 pp. $10
Symbolic, non-linear approach to the meaning of fairytale and dream motifs.

3. On Divination and Synchronicity: Meaningful Chance.
Marie-Louise von Franz (Zurich). ISBN 0-919123-02-3. 128 pp. $10
A penetrating study of time, number and methods of divining fate. Illus.

4. The Owl Was a Baker's Daughter: Obesity and Anorexia Nervosa.
Marion Woodman (Toronto). ISBN 0-919123-03-1. 144 pp. $10
The body as mirror of the psyche in eating disorders and weight problems.

5. Alchemy: An Introduction to the Symbolism and the Psychology.
Marie-Louise von Franz (Zurich). ISBN 0-919123-04-X. 288 pp. $16
Detailed guide that completely demystifies the subject. **84 Illustrations.**

6. Descent to the Goddess. A Way of Initiation for Women.
Sylvia Brinton Perera (New York). ISBN 0-919123-05-8. 112 pp. $10
Timely study of women's freedom and the need for an inner female authority.

7. The Psyche as Sacrament: C.G. Jung and Paul Tillich.
John P. Dourley (Ottawa). ISBN 0-919123-06-6. 128 pp. $10
Comparative study by Jungian analyst who is also a Catholic priest.

8. Border Crossings: Carlos Castaneda's Path of Knowledge.
Donald Lee Williams (Boulder). ISBN 0-919123-07-4. 160 pp. $12
The first thorough psychological examination of the Don Juan novels.

9. Narcissism and Character Transformation.
Nathan Schwartz-Salant (New York). ISBN 0-919123-08-2. 192 pp. $13
Draws upon a variety of analytic points of view (Jung, Freud, Kohut, etc.). Ill.

10. Rape and Ritual: A Psychological Study.
Bradley A. Te Paske (Minneapolis). ISBN 0-919123-09-0. 160 pp. $12
Incisive combination of theory, clinical material and mythology. Illustrated.

11. Alcoholism and Women: The Background and the Psychology.
Jan Bauer (Montreal). ISBN 0-919123-10-4. 144 pp. $12
New approach based on case material, dreams and archetypal patterns.

12. Addiction to Perfection: The Still Unravished Bride.
Marion Woodman (Toronto). ISBN 0-919123-11-2. 208 pp. $12
Powerful and authoritative look at the psychology of modern women. Illus.

13. Jungian Dream Interpretation: Theory and Practice.
James A. Hall, M.D. (Dallas). ISBN 0-919123-12-0. 128 pp. $12
Practical guide with many clinical examples and common dream motifs.

14. The Creation of Consciousness: Jung's Myth for Modern Man.
Edward F. Edinger, M.D. (Los Angeles). ISBN 0-919123-13-9. 128 pp. $12
An important new book by the author of *Ego and Archetype*. Explores the significance of Jung's work, the meaning of human life and the pressing need for humanity to become conscious of its dark, destructive side. Illustrated.

15. The Analytic Encounter: Transference and Human Relationship.
Mario Jacoby (Zurich). ISBN 0-919123-14-7. 128 pp. $12
A sensitive study illustrating the difference between relationships based on projection and those characterized by psychological objectivity and mutual respect. Shows how complexes manifest in dreams and emotional reactions.

16. Change of Life: Dreams and the Menopause.
Ann Mankowitz (Santa Fe). ISBN.0-919123-15-5. 128 pp. $12
A moving account of a menopausal woman's Jungian analysis, revealing this crucial period as a time of rebirth – a rare opportunity for psychological integration, increased strength and specifically feminine wisdom.

17. The Illness That We Are: A Jungian Critique of Christianity.
John P. Dourley (Ottawa). ISBN 0-919123-16-3. 128 pp. $12
A radical study by Catholic priest and analyst, exploring Jung's views that the Gnostic, mystical and alchemical traditions contain the necessary compensation for the essentially masculine ideals of Christianity.

18. Hags and Heroes: A Feminist Approach to Jungian Psychotherapy with Couples. ISBN 0-919123-17-1. 192 pp. $14
Polly Young-Eisendrath (Philadelphia)
A highly original integration of feminist views with the concepts of Jung and Harry Stack Sullivan. Detailed strategies and techniques; emphasis on revaluing the feminine and re-assessing the nature of female authority.

19. Cultural Attitudes in Psychological Perspective. 128 pp. $12
Joseph L. Henderson, M.D. (San Francisco). ISBN 0-919123-18-X.
A thoughtful new work by the co-author of *Man and His Symbols*. Examines the nature and value of social, religious, aesthetic and philosophic attitudes, showing how the concepts of analytical psychology can give depth and substance to an individual *Weltanschauung*. Illustrated.

20. The Vertical Labyrinth: Individuation in Jungian Psychology.
Aldo Carotenuto (Rome). ISBN 0-919123-19-8. 144 pp. $12
A guided journey through the analytic process, following the dreams of one man who over a lengthy period of analysis finds new life and inner purpose; an individual journey that yet echoes the universal themes of humanity.

21. The Pregnant Virgin: A Process of Psychological Transformation. Marion Woodman (Toronto). ISBN 0-919123-20-1. 208 pp. $15
A major new work about the struggle to become conscious of our own unique truth and inner potential. Explores the wisdom of the body, relationships, dreams, initiation rituals, addictions (food, drugs, work, etc.). Illustrated.

Add $1 per book (bookpost) or $3 per book (airmail)

INNER CITY BOOKS
Box 1271, Station Q, Toronto, Canada M4T 2P4   (416) 927-0355

ORDER FORM
Please detach and fill out both sides

Prices quoted are in U.S. dollars
(except for Canadian orders)

Title	Price	Copies	Amount
1. Raven	$10	_____	_____
2. Redemption	$10	_____	_____
3. Divination	$10	_____	_____
4. The Owl	$10	_____	_____
5. Alchemy	$16	_____	_____
6. Descent	$10	_____	_____
7. Psyche	$10	_____	_____
8. Border	$12	_____	_____
9. Narcissism	$13	_____	_____
10. Rape	$12	_____	_____
11. Alcoholism	$12	_____	_____
12. Addiction	$12	_____	_____
13. Dream	$12	_____	_____
14. Creation	$12	_____	_____
15. Encounter	$12	_____	_____
16. Change	$12	_____	_____
17. Illness	$12	_____	_____
18. Hags	$14	_____	_____
19. Culture	$12	_____	_____
20. Labyrinth	$12	_____	_____
21. Virgin	$15	_____	_____

Subtotal: _____

Plus Postage/Handling: _____
($1 per book or $3 per book airmail)

TOTAL: _____

Orders from outside Canada pay in $U.S.

Please make check or money order payable to
INNER CITY BOOKS

INNER CITY BOOKS
Box 1271, Station Q
Toronto, Canada M4T 2P4

Check or Money Order enclosed for _____

Please send books to:

NAME: _____

ADDRESS: _____

_____ Zip or Postal Code: _____

Please send _____ (quantity) Catalogues/Order Forms to me _____ and _____ to:

NAME: _____

ADDRESS: _____

_____ Zip or Postal Code: _____

<u>REMARKS</u>